ESSENTIAL LIFE SKILLS FOR TEEN GIRLS

A Guide to Managing
Your Home, Health,
Money, and Routine
for an Independent Life

DANI SILAS

Producer & International Distributor
eBookPro Publishing
www.ebook-pro.com

ESSENTIAL LIFE SKILLS FOR TEEN GIRLS: A Guide to Managing Your Home, Health, Money, and Routine for an Independent Life

DANI SILAS

Copyright © 2023 Made Easy Press

All rights reserved; No parts of this book may be reproduced or transmitted in any form or by any means, electronic or mechanical, including photocopying, recording, taping, or by any information retrieval system, without the permission, in writing, of the author.

Illustrations and Cover: Natalie Lukatsky

Contact: agency@ebook-pro.com

ISBN 9789655753578

CONTENTS

INTRODUCTION 5

PART 1: AROUND THE KITCHEN

CHAPTER 1: Introduction to Kitchen Appliances 9
CHAPTER 2: The Food Groups 13
CHAPTER 3: Shopping for Groceries 15
CHAPTER 4: Storing Produce 18
CHAPTER 5: Organizing Your Kitchen 21
CHAPTER 6: Meal Planning 24

PART 2: AT HOME

CHAPTER 7: Cleaning Equipment 28
CHAPTER 8: Household Maintenance Tools 32
CHAPTER 9: Cleaning a Kitchen 35
CHAPTER 10: Doing Laundry 38
CHAPTER 11: Hanging a Picture 42
CHAPTER 12: Sewing a Button 45

PART 3: PERSONAL HEALTH AND CARE

CHAPTER 13: Healthy Eating 50
CHAPTER 14: Basic First Aid 53
CHAPTER 15: Personal Hygiene 56
CHAPTER 16: Menstrual Hygiene 59
CHAPTER 17: Wardrobe Essentials 61

PART 4: MONEY AND BUDGETING

    CHAPTER 18: Planning a Budget....................66
    CHAPTER 19: Saving Up........................70
    CHAPTER 20: Insurance........................73
    CHAPTER 21: Signing a Contract..................76
    CHAPTER 22: Writing a Check....................79

PART 5: SOCIAL SKILLS

    CHAPTER 23: Emergency Contacts..................84
    CHAPTER 24: Basic Etiquette....................86
    CHAPTER 25: Navigating Social Media..............89
    CHAPTER 26: Giving and Accepting Criticism........92
    CHAPTER 27: Staying Safe......................95

PART 6: PERSONAL DEVELOPMENT

    CHAPTER 28: Time Management..................100
    CHAPTER 29: Setting Personal Goals..............103
    CHAPTER 30: Regulating Your Emotions............107
    CHAPTER 31: Creating a Support System..........109
    CHAPTER 32: Meditation and Mindfulness..........112

PART 7: WORKING

    CHAPTER 33: Writing a Résumé..................116
    CHAPTER 34: Acing an Interview..................120
    CHAPTER 35: Knowing Your Rights at Work........124
    CHAPTER 36: Starting a Business................127

CONCLUSION..130

INTRODUCTION

Growing up and gaining your independence is one of the most exciting times in your life. You're just starting to figure yourself out, you're developing hopes and dreams for your future, and you have so much to enjoy and look forward to.

However, as a teen, it's understandable if you sometimes feel frustrated that you don't yet have all the knowledge or skills you need to truly go out and take the world by storm. Schools do a good job teaching you math, science, and literature, which are all very important things to know. But what about those little things in day-to-day life that no one ever bothered to teach you?

Shopping for groceries, for instance, and storing your food properly so it stays fresh. Budgeting your money so that you are able to save up for future expenses. Even managing your own emotions or learning how to graciously accept criticism.

This book lets you take your life into your own hands and covers all the big and small things you should know as a young adult.

You can read it from cover to cover, or you can skip between select topics. In a jam and suddenly need to sew a button back onto a shirt? Jump straight to chapter 12. Having some entrepreneurial thoughts and looking for help starting your first business? Open up chapter 36. Ready to go out and get your first job but have no idea how to approach writing your résumé? Chapter 33 has exactly what you need.

That's the beauty of learning life skills – you can learn them any way at any time, and chances are all the skills in this book are ones you will put to good use some day. If not today, maybe in a year or two, or perhaps not even until you're an adult! But each and every one will enrich your knowledge and improve your ability to be a confident, self-sufficient human.

Remember – being a teenager is the perfect time to take risks and try new things. Use this book as a friendly guide to taking your first steps in the big wide world, where endless opportunity and adventure await!

PART 1: AROUND THE KITCHEN

CHAPTER 1:
INTRODUCTION TO KITCHEN APPLIANCES

The kitchen is an integral part of any home and an important thing to get to know as you become an adult. The kitchen is where you store your food and prepare your meals, so it's crucial to know your way around it.

REFRIGERATOR AND FREEZER

These are essential appliances in every kitchen. Refrigerators have a regulated temperature that is lower than room temperature, usually between 37°-41°F, and it is ideal for storing perishable foods.

This includes fruits and vegetables, dairy products such as milk, cheese, and yogurts, eggs, fresh fish and meat (if intended to be cooked soon), drinks, and condiments.

Freezers are kept at a lower temperature, usually below 0°F. Foods stored in the freezer will freeze within a few hours, so keep this in mind when planning your meals – you might have to defrost something before you can use it!

MICROWAVE

A microwave is an appliance used to defrost or heat food, and sometimes even for cooking meals. Microwaves are quick and easy to use, making them an efficient kitchen appliance. Use the time and power settings on the microwave to best heat your food. Some microwaves also have a "defrost" setting, which is perfect for quick and easy defrosting.

OVEN

Ovens are mainly used for cooking, heating food, and baking. The temperature of the oven can be set to preference and usually ranges between 200°-400°F. Lower temperatures are ideal for defrosting and heating food, medium temperatures are used for cooking and baking and higher temperatures mainly serve for short-term roasting.

Oven-safe cookware includes copper, steel, cast iron, and non-stick. Most pots, pans, and baking trays are okay in the oven. Dishes that are not oven-safe include wood, plastic, and ceramic.

Ovens have different settings, each for different uses. These are the most commonly used oven settings:

CONVENTIONAL – the oven will heat both on the top and the bottom, eliciting a uniform temperature. This setting is used for meats, bread, and some cakes.

BOTTOM ELEMENT – only the bottom element of the oven will heat up. This is good for things that need a crispy base.

FAN – this setting uses a fan to spread hot air throughout the oven. It is suitable for large dishes which need to be soft on the inside but well done on the outside, like cakes and meats that are rare on the inside.

GRILL – wavy lines indicate a grill setting, which is best for crisping and browning food. Use it for toasted sandwiches, cheesy casseroles like lasagna, and roasted vegetables.

 BOTTOM ELEMENT WITH GRILL – this is a good function for pies, quiches, and pizzas.

 FAN GRILL – the fan distributes heat evenly while the grill roasts from the top. Perfect for cooking meat and poultry.

STOVETOP

A stovetop can be gas, electric, or induction. Stovetops are used for cooking and frying in pots and pans. Gas cooktops use an open flame which can be adjusted instantly. Electric stovetops use heating elements encased in ceramic-glass surfaces, on which dishes can be placed directly. Induction stovetops use electromagnetic energy to generate heat directly within cookware, essentially making the dishes heat themselves. Induction cooktops can only be used with compatible dishes – so always check to make sure your pot or pan is induction-safe.

DISHWASHER

A dishwasher, while not found in every kitchen, is a useful time-saving appliance. It uses a mixture of water and detergent distributed by rotating sprayers, saving you the effort of hand-washing your dishes. It is important to check that your dishes are dishwasher-safe. Cast iron, wood, and non-stick are examples of what you should *not* put in your dishwasher.

When using a dishwasher, make sure to always place hollow dishes (like cups and bowls) upside down. Don't forget to load the dishwasher detergent, which can come in the form of tablets, powder, or gel. Do not use regular dish soap in your dishwasher! Next, choose the wash cycle you want – quick (for fewer dishes that are not too dirty), normal, or heavy-duty (for heavily soiled dishes).

TIPS

- When storing cooked food in the fridge, always make sure to store it in sealed containers. This will keep your fridge from picking up odors which can be hard to eliminate, and will also serve to make sure your food stays fresh for longer.
- You must never put anything with metal in it in a microwave – metal igniting in a microwave is a common cause of kitchen fires. This includes aluminum foil.
- When following a recipe that calls to use an oven, always make sure to set the mode and temperature according to the recipe's requirements.

Now you have a working understanding of the appliances in your kitchen, what each one does, and how to use them.

In the following chapters, we'll get into the next steps – knowing which food to buy and how to maintain a healthy lifestyle.

CHAPTER 2:
THE FOOD GROUPS

All of the food we eat can be categorized into five main food groups. Each food group has its nutritious benefits, and it is important to consume a balanced diet that includes all five food groups.

FRUITS

The fruit group includes all fruits and 100% fruit juice. Fruits have numerous health benefits and provide important nutrients. They can be eaten fresh, pureed, cooked, or in many other forms. You can incorporate fruit into your meals in smoothies, salads, or even fruit juices.

VEGETABLES

Vegetables are nutrient-dense and a good source of vitamins and minerals. This food group includes vegetables, beans, and legumes – like peas, lentils, and chickpeas. Incorporating vegetables into most of your meals is a nutritious, healthy habit.

GRAINS

The grains food group includes foods made from wheat, rice, oats, barley, or any other cereal grain – bread, pasta, rice, oatmeal, popcorn, and breakfast cereals are all considered grains. Grains can be whole or refined – some whole grains are whole wheat, oatmeal, and brown rice. Refined grains include white flour and white rice. Whole grains are considered a healthier choice as they contain more fiber, vitamins, minerals, and antioxidants than refined foods.

PROTEIN

Proteins are important in building muscles, cartilage, skin, and blood cells, thanks to the many nutrients they provide. Proteins fall into six sub-categories:

1. **LEAN MEATS** – like beef, lamb, veal, and pork
2. **POULTRY** – chicken, turkey, duck, etc.
3. **FISH AND SEAFOOD**
4. **EGGS**
5. **NUTS AND SEEDS**
6. **LEGUMES AND BEANS** – which are also considered part of the vegetables food group.

DAIRY

Dairy foods, like milk, yogurt, and cheese, are an important source of calcium, vitamin A, and vitamin D. They are vital for maintaining strong bones and keeping your body healthy. Milk products are popularly used in breakfast foods but can be incorporated into any meal – in salads, casseroles, sandwiches, and even hot or cold drinks.

In chapter 13, *Healthy Eating*, we will review the food groups in greater detail and learn how to put together healthy, nutritious meals that are also delicious.

CHAPTER 3:

SHOPPING FOR GROCERIES

Going grocery shopping can seem like a daunting task, especially when you shop at big supermarkets. But with the right tips and information, navigating the aisles and stocking your fridge and pantry can be a breeze!

First things first – start by making a list. Look through your fridge, freezer, pantry, and any other place you store food, and make a note of whatever you're running low on. A useful way to keep track of things that have run out or are about to run out is to keep a running list up on the fridge and document anything you notice should be restocked throughout the week. That way, you'll be less likely to miss out on important things when you prepare your final shopping list.

Don't forget to also consider any other household items you may need, such as toiletries and cleaning supplies. Dividing your list into sections such as fruits and vegetables, dairy, condiments, baked goods, freezer, and pantry can help you orient yourself when you get to the grocery store and save precious time.

Creating a menu for the coming week can help you construct your shopping list in the most efficient way. We'll talk some more about this in chapter 6, *Meal Planning*.

Next, plan a budget. Make sure your budget is flexible, as you will have different things to buy each week, but it is useful to have a ballpark figure of what you can afford to spend each week on groceries. This will help you avoid overspending and stick to what you need.

When you get to the grocery store, take a minute to figure out the layout. Ideally, you want to go through the aisles systematically and avoid running back and forth to get things you forgot. If you know in advance where each department is, it will be easier to stay focused.

Try to start with the things that will not be damaged if they are in the bottom of your cart or basket – such as freezer items and dry pantry items. Fruits, vegetables, and dairy products are best left for the end so that they can sit on top of the other groceries and avoid getting crushed.

If you're using a shopping cart, you can place eggs and other breakable things in the upper section where kids sit.

As you go through the aisles, look out for special offers or sales. Different brands can offer different prices for the same product – just always make sure to compare by price per quantity, not by overall price. You might see a jar of pasta sauce that is cheaper than another, but if the quantities are not the same it may not be a bargain after all!

Make sure to prepare your payment method in advance. Grocery shopping can be expensive, especially if you're maintaining your own home, so if you plan on paying with cash – make sure you have enough.

When checking out, try to bag your groceries in a way that will make it easier to unpack them at home. Divide your groceries according to where they will go when you get home – freezer items together, fridge items in another bag, fruit and vegetables separate, etc.

TIPS

- Don't go shopping on an empty stomach – this can lead to impulse buying which is never good for your budget.

- Make note of expiration dates when you buy dairy and meat products. You don't want to return home only to discover your milk expires tomorrow!

- Buying in bulk can save money, but make sure only to do this with non-perishable groceries.

Now that you're a grocery shopping pro, let's learn how to store all the produce you've bought to keep it fresh and tasty for longer, in the next chapter.

CHAPTER 4:

STORING PRODUCE

Storing food, and produce – fruits and vegetables – in particular, is a useful skill for any young person. It is easy to make the mistake of storing produce in the wrong way and then watching it go to waste before you can eat it. In this chapter, we'll go over the best ways to clean, cut, and store your fruits and vegetables and other perishables.

Produce can be divided into two groups – items that should be kept at room temperature, like on your counter or in the pantry, and items that need to be cooled in the fridge. Some items should start out at room temperature and then be moved to the fridge once they've ripened.

STORE AT ROOM TEMPERATURE – COUNTER OR PANTRY	STORE AT ROOM TEMPERATURE, THEN MOVE TO THE FRIDGE ONCE RIPENED	STORE IN THE FRIDGE
Onions and garlic – loose or in an open container	Pears, peaches, and plums – move to the fridge once softened	Apples – loose
Potatoes and sweet potatoes – loose or in an open container	Grapefruit and oranges – move to the fridge once softened	Ginger – in a sealed container
Bananas – loose or in an open container	Avocados – move to the fridge once softened	Fresh beets and radishes – in a sealed container, greens removed

Cucumbers – loose or in an open container	Pineapple – move to the fridge once cut	Lettuce, kale, and endives – unwashed
Lemons and limes – loose or in an open container	Tomatoes – move to the fridge once red and ripe, but still firm	Cabbage – loose, then in a sealed container once cut
		Carrots – in a sealed container
		Herbs – washed and dried, wrapped in paper, and sealed in an airtight container

Besides vegetables, some other groceries have unique storage requirements.

BREAD can be stored in a sealed container at room temperature for 1-2 days after buying. After that, it is best to keep it in the freezer – preferably pre-sliced, to make defrosting easier.

RAW MEAT, POULTRY, AND FISH should be kept in sealed containers in the fridge or freezer. Keep in the freezer for long-term storage and in the fridge for immediate use, or for defrosting pre-cooking.

COOKED FOOD AND LEFTOVERS go in the fridge in sealed containers for 3-4 days. They can also be stored in the freezer for future use.

TIPS

- To keep your refrigerator smelling fresh, empty and clean it periodically, with warm water and soap.

- To neutralize bad smells coming from your fridge, place a small bowl with baking soda on one of the shelves. The baking soda should absorb the bad smell within a few hours. Make sure that you also remove the source of the smell (most likely rotting food or fruit and vegetables that have gone bad).

- Make it a habit to go through the contents of your fridge once a week and throw out anything that is ruined.

- Label your containers in the freezer, to make them easier to identify when you want to use them.

- In the next chapter, you'll learn how to keep the rest of your kitchen – your pantry and counter – clean and organized as well.

CHAPTER 5:

ORGANIZING YOUR KITCHEN

Keeping your kitchen tidy and organized is essential, especially if your kitchen space is relatively small. There are ways to organize and put things away that will not only save you time and keep your kitchen tidy, but will also make sure your food stays fresh and in optimal condition.

Let's look at what kinds of things are stored in a kitchen. Besides food, which fills up the fridge, freezer, pantry, and sometimes some counter space, we also have appliances, cooking utensils, dishes and silverware, cookware, cleaning supplies, and more. Each thing should have its place so that you can easily find your ingredients and utensils while cooking, and replace them as needed.

WHERE SHOULD YOUR APPLIANCES GO? . . . . .

Larger appliances, like your fridge, oven, and perhaps dishwasher, stay in their place and do not move around. Smaller appliances, like microwaves, coffee machines, toasters, and kettles normally have a place on the kitchen counter. Use walls and corners on your counter to house these appliances – this will keep them out of your way and free up space for you to work. Consider storing appliances that you rarely use in cabinets, or even outside of the kitchen. Perhaps you have a waffle maker you only use on special occasions? Or a blender you use for smoothies and can put away for the winter?

HOW BEST TO ARRANGE YOUR DISHES AND COOKWARE

Cookware – pots, pans, and the like – is best stored near your oven or stovetop for easy access. You don't want to be scrambling around the kitchen when you've got dinner cooking.

Dishes tend to take up a lot of space. Try and stack your plates, bowls, and cups in an efficient, space-saving way. It's best to put them in an accessible spot – not too high or too low, because these are the things you will be reaching for the most at mealtimes.

MAXIMIZE YOUR SPACE WITH ORGANIZATION HACKS

To avoid clutter in cabinets and drawers, you can use dividers or containers labeled with their contents. Putting dividers in drawers makes things tidier and easier to find.

Try to use techniques that you feel will be efficient and useful in the long run – if you see you're not sticking to some organizational method, consider changing it with something else.

STRATEGICALLY ORGANIZE YOUR FOOD

Organizing the food in your pantry can be just as important as arranging dishes and appliances. Make sure to use your most frequently used dry products in the most accessible place in the pantry – at eye level, so you don't have to reach for it, and at the front, so you don't waste time rooting around tins and containers.

Putting your dry groceries in labeled containers is also a great way to save space and maintain order. That way, instead of your groceries remaining in oddly shaped and sometimes inconvenient packaging, you can organize everything in uniform containers that will make the most of your available shelf space.

Baskets are a great organizational hack for sorting things that come in packages – chips, chocolates, crackers, etc. Baskets help make sure everything stays in one place and doesn't get mixed up, allowing you to find things easily and avoid messy clutter.

CHAPTER 6:

MEAL PLANNING

When life starts getting busy, making a habit of planning out your meals in advance can be lifesaving. Meal planning saves you time, money, and effort – and it's so simple to do!

The idea of meal planning is that you plan out your meals – breakfast, lunch, dinner, and snacks – for the next few days or even a week, and then do your best to stick to your schedule.

You can plan your own meals or make a meal plan together with your family, whichever you prefer.

The best way to start is by deciding how far in advance you want to plan. A week is a good timeframe to start with, any longer schedule might be harder to stick to and more complicated to plan grocery shopping around.

THEN, STICK TO THESE SIMPLE STEPS:

1. Go through your supplies – what do you have in your fridge, freezer, and pantry that you can build meals around? Try to utilize what you already have on hand for at least two or three meals.

2. Create a meal planning template by making a chart for the week (or whichever timeframe you've chosen to plan your meals for). Make sure to note breakfast, lunch, and dinner on each day, and add slots for snacks if you'd like. You can create the template on your computer and then simply print it out and fill it in every week, to save time.

3. Next, fill out any meal plans you already have. Are you having lunch with your family on Sunday? Did you schedule a pizza date with a friend one evening this week? Fill those out in your template so that you remember you don't need to plan for those meals.

4. Now, make a meal list. Decide what you'd like to eat and which new recipes you'd like to try. Keep your meals balanced and healthy – you'll learn more about that in chapter 13, *Healthy Eating*.

   Consider your schedule – when will you have time to cook? Do you have any busier days that call for quick, easy dinners? Which lunches can be packed up and taken with you to school or work? Plan your meals in accordance with how busy your week is.

   Then, fill out your meal planning template with the titles of the meals you plan to eat – remember to consider the meals you can make out of the ingredients already available to you!

5. Now that you have your meals planned, it's time to make a shopping list. Go through each meal, one by one, and make a list of all the ingredients you'll need. Don't forget to consider side dishes, desserts, snacks, and drinks as well.

   Once your ingredient list is complete, go through your supplies again and see which ones you already have and can cross off the list.

6. Finally – put your list up somewhere prominent so that you an see it all the time. It will help you stay focused and organized and remind you what needs to be done and when.

Remember that if you've planned chicken for dinner, you might have to leave it out to defrost in the morning! Or maybe you want to make a complicated dish that needs to be prepared in advance.

The most important thing is to get creative! When we don't plan our meals in advance, it's easy to fall back on easier, quicker, and perhaps less healthy options. Making a meal plan and sticking to it is a recipe for a week full of meals you can truly enjoy!

TIPS

- Go online and research some new recipes you've never made before or would like to try – don't be afraid to be creative and original in the kitchen!

- Meal planning with a friend or family member can make the process more enjoyable, and maybe they can help you come up with ideas for dishes you wouldn't think of yourself.

- Invest in some airtight containers so that you can take a step up and prep your meals in advance. Meal prepping can save you even more time when you have a busier schedule.

PART 2:

AT HOME

CHAPTER 7:
CLEANING EQUIPMENT

A big part of being an adult is learning how to look after your own space and clean up after yourself. This handy introduction to the most basic and commonly used cleaning equipment and tools that can be found in almost any home is a great start.

First – tools. Here is a rundown of all the standard tools you need to keep a house clean.

BROOM AND DUSTPAN

These are essential for quick clean-ups of dry spills, or for preparing your space before vacuuming and cleaning the floor. Don't use a broom on wet spills, like water or mud, but for cleaning up spilled cereal, broken glass, or debris these are your go-to tools.

VACUUM

A vacuum is an incredibly effective tool for keeping dust at bay and eliminating dirt from the floor and other surfaces. Some vacuum cleaners are wireless while others must be connected to electricity to use. There are also automatic vacuum cleaners that work on a schedule, completely autonomously. Make sure not to vacuum up anything that can damage the machine, like shards of glass – it's better to deal with those using a broom and dustpan.

BUCKET AND MOP

Once your floors are swept or vacuumed, they need to be washed. Grab a bucket, fill it with warm water and cleaning fluid, and use your mop to distribute the cleaning solution evenly over the floor. Once the floor has been washed, it will take some time to dry. Try not to walk around on the floor when it's wet, as you can end up leaving stains that will tarnish your beautiful, clean home.

A bucket is also useful for rinsing out sponges or rags and for storing your cleaning equipment between uses.

Make sure never to use regular cleaning fluid and water on wooden parquet floors – these floors need special treatment and materials specifically designed for parquet so as not to damage the wood.

TOILET BRUSH

Toilets need to be cleaned regularly, so a designated toilet brush is an important investment. These usually come on a long handle, with a small stand where you can put your cleaning solution while using it.

GOOD SPONGES

Sponges are a versatile and incredibly useful cleaning tool. They can be used to scrub surfaces, walls, and even stubborn dirt on floors. Opt for sponges that have one rough side and one soft side, for an even more adaptable cleaning tool.

MICROFIBER CLEANING CLOTHS

These are great for picking up dust and wiping down delicate surfaces, like wood. They can also be used to clean windows, mirrors, or screens with the right cleaning solutions.

Next – cleaning solutions! There are many different types and brands, but here are some guidelines of what to use and when.

There are four different types of cleaning agents: detergents, degreasers, abrasives, and acids.

DETERGENTS

These are the most gentle solutions, and the most commonly used in homes. Detergents come in various forms – sprays, gels, powders, and more, and usually need to be added to water in order to work. These are best used for cleaning everyday spills and dirt.

DEGREASERS

These are, as their name indicates, solutions that battle grease, oils, and stubborn organic messes. You use them to clean ovens, stovetops, and even greasy cookware – although make sure your degreaser is food-safe before you use it on dishes.

ABRASIVES

These cleaning agents are more powerful than detergents and are used to clean dirt from hard surfaces. These are less common in households and are used more in commercial settings.

ACIDS

Acids can be mild or strong, but it is always best to wear gloves when using them. These are found most commonly in products used for cleaning toilets and showers, as they are very strong and can easily break down difficult stains.

TIPS

- Use gloves whenever you work with bleach or more powerful cleaning agents, to keep your hands safe and to prevent damaging your skin.

In chapter 9, we'll get right into the nitty-gritty of the proper way to clean a kitchen.

CHAPTER 8:

HOUSEHOLD MAINTENANCE TOOLS

Homes require constant love and care, and periodical maintenance work.

Some maintenance is best left to professionals who know what they are doing and are skilled at their craft, but there are certainly little maintenance jobs you can take care of around the house – things like changing light bulbs, hanging pictures and shelves, patching holes in the walls, and more.

To tackle these tasks, you need to have the proper equipment handy. Here is a list of some household tools you should have on hand in case of an emergency, and what each one can be used for.

HAMMER AND NAILS

Whether you need to hang something up on a wall or put together a piece of furniture, a hammer and nails are your number one household tool. Hammers can range in size and shape, but for simple tasks, a relatively light hammer with a regular head is perfectly sufficient. Nails are a hammer's best friend – they are long with flat heads and are meant to be hammered directly into drywall, wood, or other softer surfaces.

SCREWDRIVER AND SCREWS

You should have a screwdriver available in your toolbox at all times. The most use you will find for it is probably tightening loose screws in anything from cabinets and door hinges to furniture and kitchen appliances. Use a Phillips screwdriver when your screw has an X-shape on the top, and a flat screwdriver when you're working with a screw that has a straight line across the top.

It's best to also keep a collection of screws of different sizes, lengths, and shapes, in case you need to replace a screw that has broken or rusted, or for simple construction projects.

WD-40

WD-40 is a multi-functional oil-based formula that can be used for many things around the home. It comes in a spray can and can be used to protect tools from corrosion, lubricate squeaky hinges and wheels, loosen screws, remove rust, and more.

SPIRIT LEVEL

When hanging pictures, shelves, cabinets, or other decorative elements, it is important to make sure they are straight and parallel to the floor. A spirit level is a recommended tool for your toolbox, as it is easily utilized and very accurate. Once you've positioned what you wish to hang, simply place the spirit level on top of it and watch for the bubble. When the bubble is perfectly centered, your item is level.

TAPE MEASURE

A tape measure is a long, flexible ruler used for measuring lengths and distances. They are compact and easy to store but stretch out to anything from one to three meters for accurate and easy measuring. Its flexibility allows you to measure awkward shapes and spaces, and even around corners, making it an essential addition to your collection of household tools. Tape measures often have a metal clip attached to the end so that you can fasten them wherever you want – helpful when you're working alone!

STEP LADDER

A step ladder doesn't need much explanation – it's useful for reaching places you wouldn't be able to reach on your own. When hanging things high up on a wall or changing a light bulb on the ceiling, it's best to have a stable step ladder or stool to stand on, rather than relying on other less stable, and more dangerous, pieces of furniture.

TIPS

- Keep all of your tools tidy in a toolbox, bag, or designated drawer – this will make them easier to locate in times of need.

CHAPTER 9:

CLEANING A KITCHEN

When you think about it, the kitchen should be the cleanest, tidiest room in the house. It is the epicenter of all your food and meals and should be treated accordingly – a clean, germ-free kitchen is a healthy kitchen.

Keeping a kitchen clean is simple, as long as you know what to do and how often to do it. The lists below will tell you what you should do on a daily basis, and which more thorough jobs need to be done at least once a week.

DAILY

WASH THE DISHES AND CLEAN THE SINK

Aspire to end each day with a clean, empty sink. Dishes should be washed thoroughly and set out to dry or loaded into the dishwasher. The longer dirty dishes sit in the sink, the harder it will be to clean them later – and the smellier your kitchen will become.

Once your sink is free of the day's dishes, use a sponge with soap and warm water to scrub it clean and empty the residue from the sink drain into the trash.

WIPE DOWN THE COUNTERS

Wipe down any counters or work surfaces in your kitchen on a daily basis, using a wet cloth. If raw meat has been handled, clean that area more thoroughly to prevent foodborne illnesses.

If you want your counters and kitchen surfaces to really sparkle, you can spray them with detergent and wipe them down with a microfiber cloth.

TIDY CLUTTER

Put away anything that is not meant to stay out on the counter. This can be small appliances, dishes, tools, or even food. Make sure everything has its own neat, designated space, whether out on display or stored in a cabinet.

TAKE OUT THE TRASH

Even if the trash is not yet completely full, to avoid unwanted odors take out the trash at least daily. A lot of what is in there is food products or leftovers which, especially in a warmer climate, can go bad very quickly and lead to an unpleasant-smelling kitchen.

Don't forget to replace the bag in the trash can!

SWEEP THE FLOOR

Whether you've been cooking, baking, prepping, or eating, it's likely some crumbs or residue have found their way to the floor. Do a quick sweep of the kitchen floor daily, making sure to get into the corners and under the cabinets where dirt and debris tend to gather.

WEEKLY

MOPPING

Even if you sweep your kitchen floor every day, you should still mop it at least once a week to keep it shiny and free of dirt and grime.

WIPE DOWN SMALL APPLIANCES

Smaller appliances such as kettles, toasters, coffee machines, air fryers, and the like, need to be wiped clean every few days. Use a wet piece of paper or cloth to gently wipe them down on the outside, taking care to avoid getting any wires or electrical outlets and connections wet.

CLEAN THE KITCHEN CABINETS

Wipe down the front of the kitchen cabinets and pantry once a week to remove any drips, spills, or fingerprints. Don't forget inside the handles, too!

TIPS

- Clean as you go. Instead of waiting for the end of the day or week, clean up spills or grime as soon as you see them, wash the dishes when you're finished with your meal, and address specific cleanliness issues as they come up.
- Squirt some dish soap down the sink drain and then follow it up with some hot water to clear blockages.
- Place a small bowl with freshly-squeezed lemon juice in the microwave and set it for three minutes. Let it stand for a few more minutes and then easily wipe down the inside of the microwave.

CHAPTER 10:

DOING LAUNDRY

Laundry is one of those household chores that if you're not taught how to do correctly, you may well end up doing wrong. And doing laundry wrong often means saying a sad goodbye to treasured garments or comfy favorites. With this laundry guide for beginners and the helpful tips laid out at the end, you'll be sure to get your laundry right every single time!

SORTING YOUR LAUNDRY

Not all clothes and garments should be washed together. This is why we separate our laundry into separate loads. You can do this in advance, separating loads in different baskets throughout the week, or simply throw everything together and sort the clothes out once you're ready to put them in the washing machine.

Separating whites from colors is the first important step. White or other light-colored garments, when washed with darker clothes, can come out looking grimy, or a different color altogether. Make sure to separate white and light items from the rest.

Some garments are more delicate than others and they should be washed separately as well. These include mainly undergarments, which require a gentler wash cycle.

Other items, like delicate silks, evening gowns, wool, etc., shouldn't be washed in a machine at all – wash these by hand, per the instructions that will follow.

READING A LAUNDRY LABEL

Many pieces of clothing have labels, usually sewn into an inner seam or waistband, with specific instructions on laundering. Check these labels on new clothes to see whether they require special attention.

Here are some commonly-used laundry-related symbols, and what they mean:

 Machine wash – normal setting

 Machine wash – delicate setting

 Machine wash – below 80°F

 Machine wash – below 105°F

 Machine wash – below 120°F

 Machine wash – below 140°F

 Hand wash only

 Do not launder – dry clean only

WASHING AND DRYING

Once your laundry is sorted, you can begin. Before you load your clothes or linens into the washing machine, check them one by one to see if any have stubborn stains. Treat stains before washing by applying stain remover or simply rubbing some laundry detergent into the stain. You might want to consider washing clothes that are more seriously stained by hand. Make sure to unfold any sleeves or cuffs and separate balled-up socks before loading them.

After loading the machine, add detergent and fabric softener according to the machine's instructions. Most washing machines have dispensers in a little drawer that can be pulled out. The detergent will go in the section marked with two lines in a circle. The fabric softener compartment will be marked with a flower.

Detergent can come in the form of powder, liquid gel, or gel capsules. Capsules go directly into the drum together with the clothes.

Next, use the dial or buttons on the machine to choose the appropriate water temperature. The "normal" cycle should be fine for most clothes, but select a colder setting for delicates. Bed sheets and towels should be washed at a higher temperature as they need more of a sanitization treatment.

Take care not to overfill the machine – if the clothes don't have enough place to spin around, they won't come out clean. Leave about a quarter to a third of the space empty.

Once the wash cycle has finished, it's time to dry the clothes. You can either use a dryer or hang the garments out to dry – if the weather is warm enough to allow it.

Never put garments made of silk, leather, suede, wool, or spandex in the dryer, as these can be easily damaged or shrink!

When the dry cycle is complete, remove the clothes and fold them as soon as you can. This will reduce wrinkling and save you precious ironing time later.

HAND WASHING

Delicate or very dirty garments do better hand washed than in the laundry – and as previously mentioned, some clothes have clear instructions on them to hand-wash only.

First, find a clean sink, basin, or large bucket. Fill with lukewarm water – not too cold and not too hot, then add detergent to the mix. Place your clothes in the sink or bucket, preferably one at a time. Scrub them gently by hand, focusing on visibly stained parts. Then, rinse in cold water and observe the garment. It will usually take at least two or three times to make sure your clothes are thoroughly cleaned. Dry as normal.

TIPS

- If you're using a dryer, make sure to empty the lint trap before every use. There should be instructions on the machine explaining where the lint trap is and how to extract it.

- Use a mesh laundry bag to keep your socks together – that way, you'll never end up with single socks!

- Dryer sheets can be placed in the dryer with the clothes and give them a nice, fresh smell when they come out. You can even put used dryer sheets in your closet or sock drawer to keep them fragrant.

CHAPTER 11:

HANGING A PICTURE

Having the freedom to decorate your room or your home as you like is one of the privileges of adulthood. As you grow up, you are slowly learning your likes and dislikes and developing a sense of personal taste and style. And what better way to express your style than by putting it up on your walls?

Whether you're hanging a painting, a family photo, a certificate, or your own artwork, the guidelines for putting up a framed picture are quite simple.

First things first, decide where you want to hang your picture (or pictures). Look online for inspiration if you're thinking about assembling a gallery.

Position your frame against the wall exactly where you want it and make a mark on the wall with a pencil. You can use a measuring tape for this or do it by eye, but a good guideline is to try and center it as near to eye level as possible.

Now, assemble your equipment. Typically, a picture is hung on a single nail hammered into the wall. For this, all you will need is a hammer, nail, pencil, and spirit level. However, there are other options for hanging, which can be convenient when your artwork of choice is relatively light, when your wall is made of brick or plaster and not drywall, which is easier to work with, or when your picture frame does not have a hook. In these cases, you might want to consider hanging your picture on a wire or using adhesive hooks.

HANGING A PICTURE WITH A NAIL

Before you hammer a nail into the wall, make sure to clear the space beneath your target, moving any furniture to avoid getting dust on it. Place your nail gently against the wall, at a slight upward angle. Gripping the handle of your hammer, not too close to the head, gently tap the head of the nail, still holding onto it with your other hand.

After two or three taps, when you feel the nail is securely in the wall, let go of it to avoid injury. Keep tapping several more times until most of the nail is in the wall. If the nail sticks out too much, your picture won't lie flat against the wall. If you hammer it too far in, you won't have enough of it left outside to hang on.

Hang your picture on the nail and use the spirit level to adjust it until it is perfectly level.

HANGING A PICTURE WITH A WIRE

If your frame does not have a hook to hang it from, you can use a short wire or piece of string attached to the back of the frame. Attach two small hooks to either side of the frame, at the back near the top, and tie the string securely between them, pulling it almost taught but not quite.

Next, follow the steps above detailing how to hang a picture with a nail, and for the final stage simply rest the string on the nail instead of a hook.

HANGING A PICTURE WITHOUT A NAIL

If you don't have a hammer or nail available, or your renting contract doesn't allow you to make holes in the walls, there's always the easy solution of hanging your pictures on an adhesive hook. These can be found in most hardware stores and are very easy to use, but keep in mind that they can only support relatively light weights.

Just peel the strip of paper from behind, stick it to the wall at your desired height, and hang your picture!

CHAPTER 12:
SEWING A BUTTON

Sewing is a useful and important skill to pick up as you get ready to lead an independent lifestyle. Buttons tend to pop off clothes quite often and are pretty simple to mend once you get the hang of it, so learning how to sew them back on is a great first skill to try with a needle and thread.

When reattaching a button to a pair of pants, a button-down shirt, a cardigan, or any other piece of clothing, it is always best to use the original button, if available. If you do have the button, keep it somewhere safe until you have time to sew it back on. If the button is lost, find one that is as close to a match as possible. Sewing equipment stores have a large selection of buttons, so you should be able to find one that is similar. Prefer size over color when you have to, because a button that is a different size will not fit into the buttonhole.

Next, find a thread that is similar in color to your button. Or, if you see that the other buttons on the garment use a different-colored thread, try to match that color, instead.

Measure out a piece of thread between 20-25 inches long and thread it through your needle, pulling the end so that you have an equal length of thread on either side. Tie both ends of the thread together in a double or triple knot, depending on the fabric you intend to sew through. The more widely spaced the fabric is, the more times you will have to tie your knot to prevent it from slipping through the holes.

Before you start sewing, place the button in the right place on the fabric. You will be able to see where the right place is by the small needle holes left behind by the old button. Make sure to position it accurately, so as not to change the fit of the garment. Even half an inch either way and you can end up with clothes that are too big or too small!

Now, starting from the inside part of the garment, behind the button, push your needle up and through the fabric and into one of the button's holes, making sure to hold the button tight in place. Pull the thread all the way through until the tie catches on the other side.

Push the button back into another hole, this time from the front side of the fabric. Again, pull the thread all the way through.

Repeat this process, making sure to go through all the holes systematically.

IN A BUTTON WITH TWO HOLES, you will be going up through one hole and down through the other, consistently, like this:

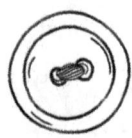

IN A BUTTON WITH FOUR HOLES, make an X pattern, as shown in the image below:

Once you've repeatedly sewn through all the holes a least four or five times and the button is firmly in place, it's time to tie off the thread. Push the needle back through so it comes out in the front of the fabric, but this time do not push it through one of the holes – bring out the needle from under the button. Now, wrap the thread around tightly a few times between the fabric and the button, this will create what is called a shank. The shank distances the button from the garment, ensuring that there is enough space for the button to fit through the hole.

Pull the needle through to the back side of the fabric again and pull tight. Tie a knot in the thread, keeping it as close as you can to the fabric. Repeat two or three times so that it's nice and tight.

Finally, use scissors to neatly cut off the remainder of the thread.

PART 3:

PERSONAL HEALTH AND CARE

CHAPTER 13:
HEALTHY EATING

Another important way to take care of yourself as a beginning adult is to take charge of your eating habits and physical health. As you become more independent, the responsibility for planning your meals and snacks and staying healthy becomes yours alone. In this chapter, you will learn the fundamentals of a balanced diet, how to plan a meal, and what different kinds of food and drink can benefit your body's physical wellness.

PUTTING TOGETHER A MEAL

A healthy, balanced plate has some of everything in it. Vegetables – whether fresh, steamed, canned, or cooked, should comprise about half of your meal. The other half of your plate should include healthy protein, preferably not processed, and grains – preferably whole. You can go back to chapter 2, *The Food Groups*, to refresh your memory about the different food groups and what is included in each.

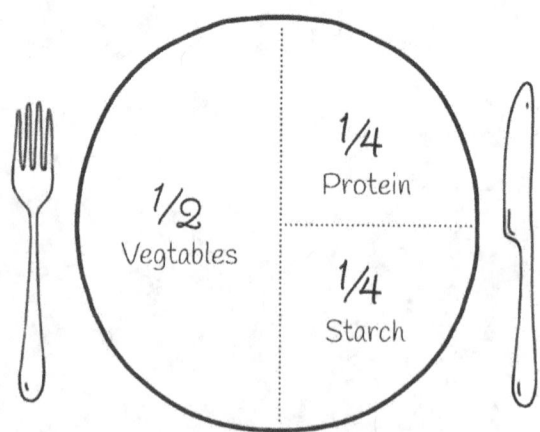

IMPORTANT NUTRIENTS

There are some key nutrients that are incredibly important to integrate into your diet during your teenage years. These nutrients help you keep strong and healthy, and are essential to your bone and muscle development.

IRON helps our cells create hemoglobin, which allows red blood cells to carry oxygen through our bodies. It can be found in proteins like meat and fish, as well as in some plant sources. If you are an active vegetarian or vegan, you'll need to get your iron from other sources so be mindful about consuming iron-rich plant-based foods, like spinach, sweet potatoes, peas, and broccoli.

CALCIUM plays an important role in strengthening bones and teeth and regulating heart rhythms. It is mostly found in dairy products like milk, yogurt, and cheese, but can also be gained through soy, tofu, and even plant-based milk.

VITAMIN D, while not sourced through food, is another crucial nutrient for young bodies. The best way to source vitamin D is through sunlight – which is why finding time to be outside is not only good for your mental health, but for your physical health as well.

HYDRATING

Hydrating regularly, or drinking water, is vital for the health of your internal organs, skin, and hair, and gives you the energy you need to function. Dehydration can lead to fatigue, weakness, muscle cramps, and more.

Remember, you might need to drink even if you don't feel thirsty – so set yourself a daily goal and try to stick to it. A recommended daily amount of water for adults is around eight cups, or more when the weather's hot.

Try to avoid soft drinks with sugar in them, which don't give you the same benefits as drinking water.

TIPS

- Eat a variety of foods – include choices from all the food groups in your meals every day.

- Be active – in addition to eating healthy, getting some activity into your daily routine is extremely important for your physical and mental health. Opt to walk shorter distances instead of driving or taking the bus, play sports as often as you can, and find ways to be active every day.

- Keep a bottle of water on or near you throughout the day to remind you to hydrate regularly.

CHAPTER 14:

BASIC FIRST AID

Knowing how to treat day-to-day injuries with basic first aid is a useful life skill. It allows us to be self-sufficient and independent, instead of relying on others for help with things that are certainly within our capabilities.

In chapter 23, *Emergency Contacts*, we'll go into greater detail about what to do and whom to call when faced with a situation you can't handle on your own, but in this chapter, we'll cover the basics of treating cuts, scrapes, burns, and fever.

ASSEMBLING A FIRST AID KIT

Every young adult should have a well-stocked first aid kit on hand in their home, for emergencies – small and big.

Equip yourself with the following things, preferably kept together in an easily accessible location in your home:

- Band-aids in a variety of shapes and sizes – for shallow cuts and scrapes
- Bandages – for deeper cuts or open wounds that require dressing
- Sterile gauze dressings, in a roll or individually packaged
- Alcohol-free cleansing wipes – for cleaning and sterilizing injuries before dressing them
- Antiseptic cream – for treating mild burns

- Antibiotic cream
- Painkillers
- A digital thermometer
- Small scissors
- Tweezers – for extracting splinters, glass shards, etc.
- Safety pins and sticky tape – for fastening dressings

TREATING CUTS AND SCRAPES

If the injury is bleeding, first clean the blood and press a clean, dry cloth to the wound until the bleeding stops. Then, clean the wound with water or a cleansing wipe and apply antibiotic cream for deeper cuts. When the wound is clean and has stopped bleeding, place a band-aid or bandage over it and secure it tightly in place. Don't forget to change the dressing once or twice a day and whenever it gets wet or dirty.

TREATING A FEVER

The average body temperature in humans is 98.6°F (37°C), and anywhere between 97° and 99°F is considered to be normal. Our body temperature can rise above regular temperature for various causes, most commonly when we are suffering from an infection.

A thermometer is the most effective tool for determining fever. If you notice that your temperature is 101.5°F or higher, or that it hasn't broken for three days, contact your healthcare provider for medical assistance.

Any fever that is lower can be managed at home – make sure to drink lots of fluids to avoid dehydration and keep warm. Painkillers with acetaminophen, ibuprofen, and aspirin can help to lower a fever if you're experiencing discomfort. Always refer to the label for dosage instructions!

TREATING MINOR BURNS

Burns can be painful, but treating them properly and soon after an injury can reduce discomfort immensely. Rinse the burn immediately under cool water for a few minutes, then put on antiseptic cream. Either leave it open to heal, or cover it with gauze if the burn is inconveniently located.

If you have lavender essential oil on hand, you can apply it to a burn and it will reduce the inflammation and relieve your pain.

CHAPTER 15:
PERSONAL HYGIENE

Maintaining good hygiene is essential to our health and makes us more pleasant to be around socially. By keeping some cleanliness habits, we can avoid exposure to infections and diseases, look good, and feel good.

WASHING

Washing with soap and water not only keeps our skin clean but reduces the risk of catching infections or spreading germs.

You should always wash your hands with soap before and after meals, after using the bathroom, after coming in contact with pets, and any other time you feel the need.

Showering or bathing should also be a daily habit (at least). It washes off the sweat and grime from a long day that you might not even notice. Make it a habit to use antiperspirants to control sweating, particularly if you know you're going to be physically active or outside a lot.

DENTAL CARE

As a teenager, you no longer have your baby teeth – all the teeth in your mouth are here to stay, or in other words, irreplaceable. So practicing good dental hygiene from a young age is necessary to keep your teeth and gums in good condition for years to come.

Brushing your teeth twice a day – morning and evening – is a must to prevent tartar from building up and plaque from hardening. In the evening before going to sleep, we brush to rid our mouths of any remains of the food we've eaten. In the morning, brushing our teeth helps our breath stay fresh for the coming day.

While brushing your teeth twice a day is important, it is not all you should be doing. Flossing at least once a day helps with gum health and removes plaque. Visit the dentist and dental hygienist regularly to keep your teeth and gums clean and healthy and identify issues that need more thorough attention.

SKIN CARE

The teenage years are characterized by changing hormones and skin issues. Having a good skincare routine can keep your skin from getting too oily and minimize the risk of severe acne.

It is important to remember that everyone's skin changes during puberty, and it is almost impossible to completely avoid some acne, blackheads, and oily skin. However, we can take measures to keep our skin as clean as possible, thus reducing the possible long-term effects of puberty on the skin and helping our skin look better day to day.

The first and most important skincare habit is washing your face daily with warm water and soap. Use face soap to thoroughly cleanse the skin on your face and neck and always remove any makeup before you go to sleep at night.

Products like cleansers and creams can go a long way to protect your skin, so consult a dermatologist about your skin type and the best product for your needs.

HAIR CARE

Different types of hair require different hair care routines – whether your hair is long or short, curly, wavy, or straight, whether you wear it up or down, it is important to incorporate a routine of washing, cleaning, and treating to ensure healthy, beautiful hair.

Regardless of hair type, here are some basic guidelines you should stick to:

- Wash your hair regularly, using shampoo and conditioner. Whether your hair is straight or curly, always detangle it after washing. For curls, using a wide-toothed comb or hairbrush can work miracles on your tangles.

- Trimming your hair regularly, every six months at least, can contribute to healthier, faster-growing hair and prevent split ends, which stunt hair growth.

- Whenever possible, prefer heatless hairstyling methods. Heat, when used directly and regularly, is damaging to hair. When you do use heat-styling tools, applying a heat protection serum first will go a long way to protect your hair from damage.

- Your hair needs good nutrition and sleep just as much as your body does! Your locks will thank you for drinking sufficient water and maintaining a balanced diet and sleep schedule.

CHAPTER 16:
MENSTRUAL HYGIENE

Menstruation is a normal biological part of growing up, which usually begins between the ages of nine and fifteen and continues monthly through all your fertile years.

Getting your period can be a scary thing, especially when you don't know exactly what it means or how to handle it. It is important to remember that your period is completely natural – and almost every girl and woman around you experiences it, too. Every month, your uterus prepares itself for a potential pregnancy. If you do not get pregnant, your body begins its menstruation cycle, shedding the lining it built only to rebuild it again the following month. A typical menstrual cycle lasts 28 days, and the period of menstrual bleeding usually lasts 2-6 days.

Menstruation is sometimes accompanied by painful cramping and mood swings, due to changing hormone levels in your body. Maintaining good menstrual hygiene is key to your general health and comfort during this time.

There are all sorts of different menstrual products which you can use. Different things work for different people, so you may want to experiment some before settling on what suits you best:

- **PADS** – these are padded strips that attach to the inside of your underwear to absorb the blood. They come in different sizes, depending on flow.

- **TAMPONS** – these are thin absorbent tubes inserted to absorb blood before it flows out of your body. They can take some time to get used to and come in varying sizes, too. Tampons need to be changed often, no less than every eight hours.

- **MENSTRUAL CUP** – the menstrual cup is inserted like a tampon and is made of a flexible material. These can be extracted, cleaned, and then inserted again several times a day. A menstrual cup is a more eco-friendly choice than disposable products but requires you to clean it thoroughly between uses.

- **PERIOD UNDERWEAR** – if you are uncomfortable using pads or tampons, you can buy period underwear made from ultra-absorbent material. These are more recommended for lighter flow and can be washed and laundered like regular underwear.

CHAPTER 17:
WARDROBE ESSENTIALS

It doesn't matter if you're at school, going out with friends, running errands, or interviewing for a job, being mindful of how you look and dress is a big part of the impression you make on others.

We've all felt like we have nothing to wear or spent hours staring blankly at our full closet. The trick to easily put together an outfit for any occasion is building a basis of essential pieces of clothing, which you can mix and match and add to as needed.

These are some of the must-haves for every girl's closet:

BASIC BLACK AND WHITE T-SHIRTS

These are an excellent base piece for any outfit. You can dress them up with fitted pants and a blazer, or down with jeans and a jacket – the plain tee is a versatile piece of clothing to invest in.

JEANS

Jeans, though on the casual side, are essential for any teen girl. Make sure the fit and length are right for you and that they are comfortable enough to spend a day in. Great for school, errands, going out, or staying in – a good pair of jeans is a must.

TAILORED PANTS

Whenever you find yourself in a situation where the dress code is more business than casual, a pair of tailored pants will do the trick every time. Black is classic, but you can make navy, beige, gray, and even pinstriped work as well. Matched with a T-shirt or blouse, and paired with a blazer for an elevated look, tailored pants are essential to your wardrobe.

A BLACK DRESS

Simple but classic, the plain black dress can be worn on almost any occasion. Layers and accessories can add to your look, changing it up to fit your mood and the dress code.

A SUMMER DRESS

A summer dress is the perfect casual attire for warm days. Loose and flowy, it makes for comfortable wear and is a no-fuss solution for busy mornings. Grab a cardigan with you for colder evenings or air-conditioned buildings, and pair it with sandals, flip-flops, flats, or heels to suit your destination.

EVERYDAY SNEAKERS

Sneakers are a perfect solution for almost any time of year – comfy, trendy, and basic, a good pair of sneakers in white or another neutral color can go well with almost anything you wear – short or long, formal or casual, warm or cool.

MATCHING AN OUTFIT

Here are some basic guidelines for putting together an outfit that matches:

- Choose one piece that is your statement piece and work around it – it can be a top, pants, shoes, accessory, or anything really. Set up the rest of your outfit with more muted garments to make your statement piece pop.

- Combine loose with tight – if you're going for a flowy or oversized top, choose a more fitted pair of pants or a pencil skirt. If you opt for flared or wide-legged jeans or pants, pair them with a form-fitting top.

- Experiment with layers – layering can give a look more depth, so try putting a button-down under a sweater or adding a jacket to a summer dress.

- Know which colors match – avoid pairing black with other dark colors like brown or navy, or bright colors with other bright colors. Make sure to have some neutral-colored pieces to combine with brighter ones.

PART 4: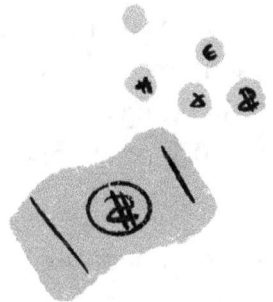
MONEY AND BUDGETING

CHAPTER 18:
PLANNING A BUDGET

Learning how to make a budget and stick to it is a great skill to master when preparing for adulthood. Being financially responsible and knowing how to manage your expenses will make adulting that much easier once you're living away from home, and supporting yourself.

The first, and most important thing, is to figure out your income and expenses.

INCOME is all the money that you acquire or earn – from work, allowance, gifts, etc.

EXPENSES refer to the total sum of money you spend in a given time.

It's common to look at income and expenses on a monthly or weekly basis, so start by figuring out your average monthly or weekly cash flow – whichever you prefer.

You can divide each into categories, putting together a table that looks something like this, but customized to your own needs:

INCOME (MONTHLY)

CATEGORY	AMOUNT ($)
Allowance	
Work	

Gifts	
Other	
TOTAL	

EXPENSES (WEEKLY)

CATEGORY	AMOUNT ($)
Gas	
Entertainment	
Beauty and grooming	
Other	
TOTAL	

Once you've filled out the tables, subtract your total expenses from your total income. If you're left with a positive value, that means your expenses do not exceed your income and you are managing to save some money. If the value is negative, that means you're overspending your income.

Tracking your habits like this, on a weekly or monthly basis, is the first step to becoming financially conscious. When you are intentional about how much you make and spend, you can be responsible with your money and know where you should be cutting down your spending and by how much.

After figuring out your total monthly spending pattern, you can take measures to reduce expenses in the next months.

Budgeting means deciding in advance how much you are willing or able to spend on certain expenses while taking into account the income you receive.

Your expenses can be categorized into three types: **NECESSARY**, **EXTRAS**, and **SAVINGS**.

Your necessary expenses are the ones that you cannot avoid – gas, groceries, tuition, etc.

Extras are luxuries you allow yourself (which are important as well) – eating out, entertainment, travel, shopping, etc.

Savings refers to the money you put away, not to be used. You can learn more about saving money in the next chapter.

To set your budgeting goals, outline a realistic monthly or weekly budget for each type of expense in the "extras" category, as these are the ones you have control over.

You may decide to cut down on takeaway meals, or bike to school instead of taking public transport. You might limit yourself to a certain amount of money you can spend on clothes each month, or opt for cheaper options when choosing where to eat.

THIS PART IS UP TO YOU – BUT REMEMBER THESE IMPORTANT GUIDELINES:

- Try to budget in a way that will balance your income and expenses so that you are not overspending.

- Once you've decided on a budget you'll have to stick to it. So make your plans realistic and achievable.

- Consider ways to increase your income if you see that it is not enough to cover your expenses – you can find odd jobs like babysitting or tutoring, or get a steady job you can commit to over time.

CHAPTER 19:

SAVING UP

Having a budget and sticking to it is great preparation for adult life, and a first step toward financial stability. But if you feel ready to take your finances one step further and also secure some funds for your future, you need to understand the basics of saving.

You might want to start saving up for your college tuition, your first car, or simply put away some money for anything you may one day need. Either way, you'll find that money gets spent easily, without you even noticing, when it is there in your wallet or sitting in your bank account.

The idea behind saving is putting a certain sum of money away where it is not as readily available to spend and letting that money accumulate over time. Developing good savings habits as a teenager, when you don't yet have many financial obligations, can be a life-changing skill!

TO START SAVING, YOU'LL NEED THREE THINGS:

1. A job or other steady income
2. Somewhere to put the money – in a physical place or a savings account in the bank
3. A plan

DECIDE WHERE YOUR MONEY WILL BE

Most banks offer teenagers savings accounts without a monthly fee. Ask your parents which bank services they use or research local banks and their benefits. Some savings accounts also offer interest, which means that the money you have in the account will earn interest at a certain rate determined by the bank, according to the deposited sum and how well you can negotiate your terms.

Alternatively, if you're saving for a more immediate goal and you receive your allowance or salary in cash, you may just want to put some money aside in a safe place at home until you have enough to spend.

INCREASE YOUR INCOME AND DECREASE YOUR SPENDING

Even if your parents give you an allowance or if you're earning money from odd jobs or a regular gig, there are always ways to increase your income. The more you earn – the more you can save! You can pick up a summer job, create things and sell them, or utilize your skills to secure some freelance work. If you have an idea for a business venture and an entrepreneur's spirit, go to chapter 36, *Starting a Business*, to learn the basics of starting your own business!

Another way to save money is to decrease your spending. You can refer back to chapter 18, *Planning a Budget*, for ways of being more frugal with your finances.

SET A GOAL AND MAKE A PLAN

Your goal can be specific – for example, you want to save enough money for a big trip after graduation. In this case, your goal will have a desired sum and a deadline. Your goal can also be general – save X amount of money every month, or Y percent of your income every month. Either way, having a goal in mind will keep you motivated to stick to your savings plan.

Saving money has to be a deliberate effort. Make a systematic plan that fits your income and is realistic with regard to your goals. Consider your regular expenses and don't overestimate how much you can reasonably save, because you don't want to find yourself in a situation where you are unable to meet your weekly or monthly goal. Calculate your income and expenses and see how much there is left to put away.

Once you have a specific number in mind, break down your goal and turn it into a habit. It can be daily, weekly, or monthly, or it can even be automated if you're working with a bank account, but it should be something that is cemented into your financial mindset and considered just another one of your necessary expenses – that way, you'll be more likely to stick to your goal.

CHAPTER 20:
INSURANCE

Insurance is a system that compensates you for unexpected loss or damage of anything of value – a car, home, pet, valuable items, your health, or even life. People have insurance for all sorts of things, but the idea behind them all is the same. You pay an insurance company a set sum called a *premium* – it can be weekly, monthly, yearly, etc., and in the event that you suffer loss or damage to whatever is covered by your insurance agreement, the insurance company helps you cover the expense of your loss.

Say your parents have home insurance, for example, and one winter it rains so heavily that the house floods. Because your parents have been paying an insurance company over the years, they are entitled to file an *insurance claim* to receive the money they need to fix the roof and ceiling and replace whatever furniture has been ruined, in accordance with the terms of the agreement they signed and so long as the agreement is still valid.

Insurance policies have a *policy limit*, which is the maximum amount the company is willing to pay for a particular loss. Some policies will require a *deductible* – a certain sum that you must pay yourself to help cover the loss before the insurance company covers the remainder. This means that if the loss or damage is relatively small and inexpensive and does not exceed your agreed-upon deductible, your insurance policy may not contribute to it at all.

The cost of insurance varies depending on the type and other factors. It is not usually mandatory to have insurance, and often you pay insurance companies money that you will never see again. Still, not having insurance is a risk that should be considered carefully in light of what you have to lose.

MAIN TYPES OF INSURANCE POLICIES........

- **HOME INSURANCE** – home insurance can compensate you for damage to your home and the theft of its contents. Home or renters' insurance is usually a requirement and should be considered in your expenses when you start thinking about moving into your own place.

- **AUTO INSURANCE** – a car or other automobile is an expensive asset and as such should be protected. Auto insurance can help cover the cost of damage sustained to your car in an accident or even just regular maintenance, and it can also cover damage sustained by other people and automobiles in an accident in which you are involved.

- **HEALTH INSURANCE** – health insurance allows its policyholders all sorts of benefits when it comes to healthcare. Depending on the policy, it might cover special treatments, medications, or medical attention, or give access to cheaper and more available medical care. The cost of health insurance is tailored to each policyholder and tends to be more expensive when the person has a chronic health issue or is more likely to need specialized medical aid.

- **LIFE INSURANCE** – in the tragic event of someone's death, life insurance in their name guarantees that the insurance company pays a fixed sum of money to the deceased's next of kin or whichever beneficiary is named in the policy. This sum can help cover funeral expenses or debts left by the deceased.

- **TRAVEL INSURANCE** – traveling to a foreign country or even domestically can often involve fees you may not have considered in advance. Things like loss of luggage, medical attention in a country where you do not have health insurance, loss or theft of valuable items like a phone, laptop, or jewelry, or the unexpected cost of accommodations due to a delayed flight, are all things that can be covered in a travel insurance policy. These policies are short-term and valid only for the duration of your travels and mostly require a one-time payment and not a regular premium.

Insurance, in short, is a risk management practice. Just like with other contracts, which you can read more about in chapter 21, *Signing a Contract*, it is important to know exactly what your insurance policy covers and whether your premium is consistent or can change over time. Understanding the different types of insurance and their pros and cons can help you decide which premiums are worth their cost, and which can be omitted.

CHAPTER 21:

SIGNING A CONTRACT

Contracts are signed legal documents that bind their parties to the terms and obligations of a specific agreement.

When you put your signature on a contract, you are committing to uphold your end of the agreement, whatever that may be. Often, contracts center around financial obligations, but really, they can pertain to anything.

WHAT DOES IT MEAN WHEN YOU SIGN A CONTRACT?

A signature is a unique, personal mark. They often include a part of a person's name, but they don't have to. Ideally, your signature should be simple, quick, and easy to recognize. The idea behind a signature is that it is something only you should know how to replicate perfectly, which is why it is used on legal documents to prevent fraud. Imagine if everyone's signature was simply the first letter of their last name – anyone could replicate anyone else's signature, and sign contracts unknowingly on their behalf!

When you put your signature on a contract, it means that you have read, understood, and agreed to everything stated in the contract – and you know that if you should fail to uphold your side of the agreement, you might face legal consequences.

Sometimes, these documents can be long, complicated, and difficult to read. However, it is important to learn how to properly read a contract to ensure that you know exactly what you're agreeing to.

HOW TO APPROACH A CONTRACT............

There are all sorts of situations when you may be asked to sign a contract. For example, when you start a new job, often your employer will require that you sign a contract detailing your terms of employment, salary, work hours, and other obligations to your place of work. The document should also include your employer's obligations to you – benefits, overtime, PTO (paid time off) and sick days, etc.

When you rent your first apartment or buy a home you will be required again to sign a contract with all the information about the transaction between you and your landlord.

The first few times you sign a contract, you should ask a trusted adult to look over it with you. They can point out important things you may not have discussed verbally with the other party, or recommend changes to the wording or details. If there is something in the contract you are uncomfortable with, you can always check whether it is open for negotiation.

Always read through the entire thing. It can seem long and tedious, but reading everything – even the small print – is incredibly important. You don't want to end up discovering that you've agreed to something you were unaware of.

Once you've signed a contract, make sure to have a copy. It can be physical or digital, but keep it somewhere safe just in case you need to refer back to it one day, or for a situation where you encounter legal issues that need sorting out.

WHEN SHOULD YOU NOT SIGN A CONTRACT?

YOU SHOULDN'T SIGN A CONTRACT IN THE FOLLOWING SCENARIOS:

1. You feel pressured or coerced to sign. Contracts are mutual agreements and as such should be entered willingly by both parties.

2. You feel uncomfortable or unsure about one or more of the clauses. Take the time to understand exactly what you're signing and ask an adult for advice. Once you sign a contract you are legally bound to it, so it's smart to iron out any kinks before you put your name down.

3. You don't know what's in it. Never sign an agreement blindly – even if you've been told verbally what the contract contains, remember that what binds you is what is in writing, so it is crucial to know exactly what you're committing to!

CHAPTER 22:

WRITING A CHECK

Money makes the world go round, and in today's world, there are so many ways to make financial transactions. Checks are a relatively old, even outdated form of payment – they're physical and not digitized, require you to fill out the details by hand, and you need to have them readily available. Still, some businesses or establishments require their payments to be made in checks, and it sometimes works out cheaper than other payments, as paying by credit or using cash apps can carry a fee. As a teen, it's quite possible you've seen one but have never actually been taught how to use it. Writing and using checks is super simple- and requires just a few short steps!

A check draws money from your personal checking account in the bank and must be deposited by its beneficiary in order to complete a transaction. The payment is not made when you write the check and hand it over, rather it is completed only once the check has been deposited, and never before the date stated on it.

A STANDARD CHECK LOOKS LIKE THIS:

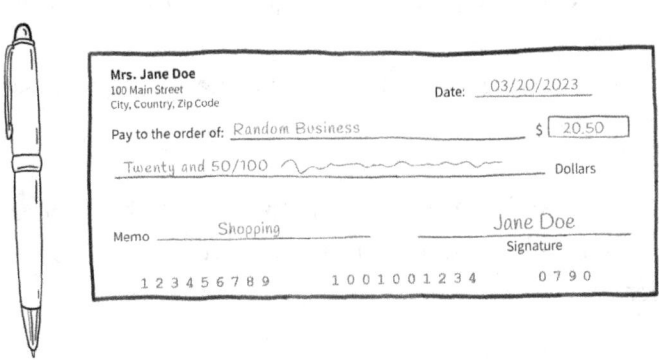

- **DATE**: write out today's full date, or a future date on which you wish the transaction to be completed. Make sure the beneficiary of your check is aware of any delay in the date.

- **PAY TO THE ORDER OF**: here, put the full name of the person or business you are paying. Always check to ensure that you have the correct spelling, as even a minor mistake can prevent the bank from accepting the check when it is deposited.

- **AMOUNT (NUMERIC)**: next to the dollar sign, in the box, write the full sum in numbers, including cents in decimals.

- **AMOUNT (WORDS)**: on the line, copy out the same amount, this time in words. Cents are denoted as a fraction – X/100, like in the example. Double-check that both numbers match. If there is an empty space between the end of your number and the end of the line, it is smart to fill in that space with a line or scribble to avoid anyone adding text. Say you wrote out a check for ten dollars and simply wrote "ten" without filling in the empty space, someone might decide to add the word "thousand" after, which you definitely don't want.

- **MEMO/FOR**: this is where you write a short memo of what you are paying for – for example, rent, groceries, loan, gift.

- **SIGNATURE**: place your unique signature on the line, as proof that the check really was written by you and is not fraudulent, and to show that you allow the check to be deposited.

That's all!

Remember to keep your own record of the checks you've written inside your checkbook so that you can easily keep track of your expenses.

TIPS

- Avoid signing blank checks. A blank check with your signature in someone else's hands can be disastrous, as they have full control to decide who can cash in the check and how much it is worth.

- Don't leave any blank spaces on your check, for the same reason.

- Write clearly and always use a pen (not a pencil) when writing out a check. Checks that are unclear can bounce, or worse, be misinterpreted.

- Double-check everything before you hand over the check.

PART 5:
SOCIAL SKILLS

CHAPTER 23:

EMERGENCY CONTACTS

Knowing how to act in an emergency is an important skill to learn. It is always better to be safe than sorry, so having a list of emergency contacts ready and knowing whom to call in what situation can make all the difference if you ever find yourself or someone else in need of urgent help.

Here is a list of contacts you should write down or save in your phone for emergencies:

- **911** (112 in Europe, or your country's equivalent) – dialing this number will direct you to an operator with the resources to dispatch any help you may need. This number is only to be dialed in emergencies – including immediate medical risk, life-threatening situations, crimes in progress, fires, car accidents, or any situation where you feel that you or someone else is in immediate danger. It is essential to provide the operator with as much information as possible so that they can dispatch the appropriate response – police, firefighting, or medical services.

- **YOUR PARENTS OR CARETAKER** – have these numbers easily accessible, and preferably know them off by heart, to quickly dial or dictate to others in emergencies.

- **POISON CONTROL** – numbers may differ according to your region. Call poison control when you know or suspect that someone has or may have come into contact with any form of poison – this includes overdosing on medication and venomous bites or stings, as well as ingesting poisonous substances.

- **LOCAL POLICE STATION AND LOCAL FIRE DEPARTMENT** – while during an emergency it is always to best to dial 911 or its equivalent, save these numbers to use when you need general help or information that is not immediate.

- **VETERINARIAN** – whether you have a pet or not, having your local veterinarian's number on hand is useful for helping animals who are lost, injured, or require other medical assistance.

- **MENTAL HEALTH SERVICE** – depending on where you are, there are local or national hotlines you can call when you feel you are in need of immediate mental health or emotional support. These hotlines can direct you to someone you can talk to, or in case of emergency dispatch appropriate help. Make sure to locate and have a number available in case you or anyone you know ever needs help.

CHAPTER 24:

BASIC ETIQUETTE

Etiquette goes beyond just "please" and "thank you" and sitting straight at the dinner table. Good manners indicate to others that you are polite and care about how you look and sound, and simply make you more pleasant to be around.

COMMUNICATING WITH OTHERS

When meeting someone new, introduce yourself or ask to be introduced by someone else. Sharing your name and perhaps some information about you can make people feel more comfortable in a social setting.

A handshake is appropriate in more formal settings or when meeting with adults, but in casual settings or among friends a simple introduction and some small talk can suffice.

Try to adapt your language per the situation. Slang and colloquialisms are fine among your peers, but some situations require more refined speech – so learn to recognize these and choose your words accordingly.

GOING OUT

When you're invited over to someone's house or to an event that is more formal than a simple get-together (such as a birthday, housewarming, dinner party, or celebration), bringing a small gift can go a long way to show that you appreciate being invited. Usually, a lot of work goes into planning and organizing these events, so a token of appreciation will always be happily received.

Consider bringing flowers, a housewarming gift (when appropriate), or even offering to help with arrangements or asking if you can bring some food or drinks. Don't bring food to a host's house without coordinating it beforehand (unless, of course, it's a close friend or this is an accepted practice in your social group), as this can be perceived as impolite.

Always express your gratitude for being hosted before you leave, making it a point to thank your host personally and compliment some element of the event.

DINING OUT

When dining out, there are some basic etiquette guidelines to adhere to.

Always be polite to your server. This will not only increase your chances of getting good service, but it will make your experience and that of the establishment's staff far more enjoyable. Remember that jobs in the service industry are often held by teenagers like you and your friends, so keep that in mind when imagining how you would like to be treated if the roles were reversed.

When eating with other people, it is polite to wait for everyone to be served before eating. This makes for a more pleasant meal and prevents awkward situations where some people are still eating while others have long since finished.

Tipping is considered a norm and, in most establishments, it is unacceptable to leave without tipping. If you are not satisfied with your service, there are alternative ways of expressing your dissatisfaction. You can phone the business later and inform them of your experience or write to them on their website or email. Most businesses will be happy and willing to hear your honest review, as long as it is communicated in a mature, genuine way.

MAINTAINING GOOD HYGIENE AND DRESSING RIGHT

How you look, sound and even smell can have a big impact on how you are perceived by others and are a big part of the unspoken language of etiquette.

To learn more or revisit the subject of personal hygiene, you can go back to chapter 15, *Personal Hygiene*.

WHEN OUT IN PUBLIC, AVOID THE FOLLOWING BEHAVIORS:

- Picking your nose
- Sneezing without covering your nose and mouth
- Saying rude or hurtful things to others
- Ignoring people when they talk to you
- Scrolling on your phone while holding a conversation or during a meal
- Being late without letting someone know in advance

CHAPTER 25:

NAVIGATING SOCIAL MEDIA

One of the most prominent characteristics of the 21st century is globalization and, with it, the rise of social media. Much of our communication is held through screens and online, and much of our time is occupied with various apps and media platforms.

Social media can be a wonderful thing – it can inspire, connect, teach, and bring people together. However, it is also something to be wary of, and learning to use it right is a crucial skill for the modern teen.

The most important thing to keep in mind when you decide to engage with this content is that there is a strong element of choice in what people present to the world. Some accounts may be more candid than others, and certainly, many people choose to use their social media personas to provide a refreshing and authentic experience for viewers. But even then, the act of creating social content is thought out and calculated. Remember, social media is not a mirror of real life.

Here are some things to look out for when engaging with social content:

ONLINE SAFETY AND PRIVACY

It is easy to unintentionally share private or personal information online. Be mindful of this, and make sure never to share your personal address or information with people you do not know and trust, or on a public platform.

Be wary of other users reaching out through comments or private messages, particularly if they are asking for information or encouraging you to meet with them. If something doesn't feel right to you – trust your instincts!

Most platforms allow you to change the privacy settings to help you control who sees your information, photos, and videos. Consult with your parents or a trusted adult on how to manage your privacy settings.

Similarly, remember that other people's private information is not yours to share – respect others' privacy like you would want them to respect yours.

CYBERBULLYING

People express themselves more freely – positively and negatively – from behind the protection of a screen. This makes it easier to make hurtful or insulting comments without having to face social consequences.

If you see something like this, targeting you or anyone else, you can report the user. Don't hesitate to block or unfollow content that makes you feel uncomfortable or upset.

Be conscious of the power you wield on your social media accounts as well – always think before you comment or post and be considerate of other people's feelings.

MENTAL HEALTH

With all the wonderful benefits of social media, we can sometimes not realize how it's affecting our mental health. Spending too much time in the magical world of TikTok or Instagram can be dangerously time-consuming, and even has the power to affect your self-confidence, happiness, and productivity.

Try to limit the amount of time you spend online – and designate times and places which are strictly social media-free. This could be mealtimes, family time, evenings before you go to sleep, outings with friends, time designated for studying, or any other setting you deem appropriate.

CHAPTER 26:
GIVING AND ACCEPTING CRITICISM

Being open to change and improvement is an important quality to learn from a young age, and how better to improve than with the help of others?

Accepting criticism doesn't always come naturally to us, especially when we tend to take things personally or when criticism is given in a negative way. In this chapter, we'll dive into the difference between constructive and destructive criticism and learn how to give criticism to others without being hurtful and how to accept it ourselves.

CONSTRUCTIVE VS. DESTRUCTIVE CRITICISM..

"Criticism" is the art of judging and defining something or someone's qualities or merits. It is not necessarily a negative thing but can be used positively or negatively depending on the content, tone, context, and other criteria.

Destructive criticism is feedback that is given for the sake of being negative. It is not used to help someone learn or improve and does not usually lead to an effective outcome.

On the other hand, *constructive criticism* is a tool used to promote positive change. It is feedback that is supported with examples and suggestions for growth.

HOW TO GIVE CONSTRUCTIVE CRITICISM

In certain situations, you might find yourself wanting to or required to comment on someone else's work or results. Follow these ground rules for giving criticism that is constructive:

- Don't only make negative comments. Focus on what needs improvement but make a note also of things that you thought were done well.

- Do not give feedback on someone's traits or personality – instead, address actions, behaviors, or decisions.

- Make suggestions on what the person can do better next time – this will ensure that your feedback is actionable.

- Make it clear that your feedback is based on your opinion and is not necessarily an objective truth. Phrases like "I think" or "maybe" can support this.

- Think over your criticism before you deliver it and get your points straight and practical.

HOW TO RECEIVE CRITICISM

Even if you make it a habit to always deliver your criticism in a positive, constructive way, you can't control how other people deliver theirs. What you do have control over is how you accept negative criticism, and what you learn from it.

- Never take it personally. Realize that feedback, however it is given, is an opportunity to learn and grow.

- Even if you feel that the criticism is unjustified, don't immediately object. You might see things differently, so take a deep breath and only then try to ask questions to better understand the criticism that was given.

- Improve. Criticism is often difficult to accept because we take it to heart. That's okay and completely natural, but getting past the insult and leveraging what you've learned to be even better is the true art of accepting criticism.

CHAPTER 27:

STAYING SAFE

As a young woman, there are measures you can take to protect yourself at home, outside, and on the road – measures that might seem unnecessary or even excessive at first but can serve to keep you safe in times of need.

Although we would like to believe it, not everyone out there is kind and law-abiding, and it is easier to take advantage of people when they are unprepared.

STAYING SAFE AT HOME

Always keep your front door locked. Certainly at night while you are sleeping, but also when you are home alone. This is a habit that is so easy to uphold and can be truly lifesaving!

Similarly, if you ever lose your keys in a public place, even though you might have neighbors or family members with keys you can copy, it is always best to change your locks and make new copies of your keys. Anyone could find a lost key and it might not be so hard to figure out where you live, particularly if the key was lost close to home or along with other identifying items.

Consider taking a self-defense course, even with a friend – self-defense is an important life skill and even just a couple of classes can give you an advantage in a struggle.

STAYING SAFE OUTSIDE

If you're walking alone in an isolated area or after dark, be alert. Don't scroll on your phone but do have it in your hand in case you need to call for help. If you're wearing earbuds, take one of them out so that you can hear any potential danger approaching.

When you go out with friends, make an agreement that wherever you go together – you leave together. Don't leave your friends behind in places that can be unsafe.

Avoid going out alone, but if you have to, let someone you trust (preferably an adult) know where you are, even if just through a text or in a note. If anything happens to you, it will be easier for them to track you down and call for help.

As a general rule – listen to your gut! If you feel threatened, unsafe, or even just uneasy about being somewhere or with someone, don't ignore that feeling.

STAYING SAFE ON THE ROAD

Always wear your seatbelt and never *ever* text and drive, or drive under the influence of drugs or alcohol. Besides it being illegal and likely to lead to your arrest, these behaviors put you, your passengers, and other people on the road in serious danger.

Remember that as responsible as you are, you can't always trust other people on the road to be as safe. Always scan intersections before driving through them and keep a sufficiently safe distance while driving behind other vehicles.

At night, when possible, park in well-lit or busy areas that are easy to navigate on your return.

STAYING SAFE IN YOUR RELATIONSHIP

Recognizing red flags in romantic relationships is so important. Look out for signs of violence or abuse in your own partner and in your friends' relationships. Here are some unhealthy and toxic behaviors that should stand out to you:

- Pressuring a partner to do things they are uncomfortable with. In a healthy relationship, you should feel safe and protected.
- Controlling a partner's social life or social media.
- Extreme jealousy.
- Physical abuse – bruises, cuts, burns, or even just guarded and indifferent behavior can be indicators of physical abuse by a partner.
- Emotional abuse – this is often much harder to recognize because it manifests beneath the surface and can escalate slowly. Behaviors like humiliation, derogatory name-calling, patronizing, yelling, belittling, dismissiveness, and gaslighting are all red flags of emotional abuse.

If you suspect that you or someone you know may be in an abusive relationship and are unable to extricate yourself from the situation, there are people who can help. Confide in a trusted adult, or reach out to a local hotline or law enforcement that can advise you on what to do and how to extract yourself from the relationship in a safe way.

To learn more about staying safe and guarding your privacy online and on social media, go back to chapter 25, *Navigating Social Media*.

PART 6:

PERSONAL DEVELOPMENT

CHAPTER 28:
TIME MANAGEMENT

School, hobbies, work, friends, and extracurricular activities can make for a busy, and sometimes even stressful, timetable. There's so much to do and so few hours in the day to do it in, and it's easy to feel overwhelmed. That's where managing your time efficiently and effectively comes in.

Time management is the skill of planning and prioritizing, and when mastered, it can make a real difference in your life.

MAKE A LIST

First things first – get everything down on paper or in a digital file. When our brain is too full, we're bound to forget something! So keeping a running list, or making a new one every day, week, or even month, will help keep your time in order. You can organize your tasks by type, and even put in things that aren't necessarily "tasks", but that you'd like to make time for – like hobbies, exercising, meeting with friends, etc.

PRIORITIZE

Once you've got a list of the things you need to do, the Eisenhower Matrix can be an extremely useful tool when deciding which ones to do first.

IT WORKS LIKE THIS:

Each task can be ranked on two scales – urgency and importance. For each thing on your list, decide whether it is urgent or not, and whether it is important or not. Remember – important is not necessarily objective! Something that someone else might rank as unimportant could be important to you.

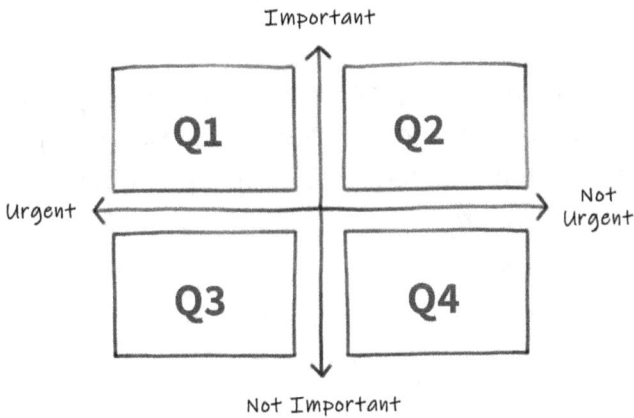

For example, a school paper that is due tomorrow is urgent and important, so that will go in Quadrant 1.

Going out to buy a gift for a friend whose birthday is in a week is important, but not urgent – put it in Quadrant 2.

The numbering of the quadrants tells you exactly how to prioritize your tasks. Start with Quadrant 1, urgent and important – do these things as soon as possible. Then, go on to Quadrant 2, important but not urgent. This might include exercising, reading, meditating, or anything else that is important to you but not time-sensitive. Fit these into your schedule whenever you have time to spare. Quadrant 3, not important but urgent, are things that you may be able to delegate to others. If not, schedule these for specific times, according to their deadline. Anything that goes into the final quadrant, not urgent and not important, should be crossed off your list. If it's not time-sensitive and it's not important to you, just don't do it – save your time for other more relevant tasks.

KEEP A SCHEDULE

Keeping a schedule is a good way to make sure your time is managed efficiently and no important things slip your mind. Use a calendar or a time-management app to monitor your tasks and prioritize like a pro.

CHAPTER 29:
SETTING PERSONAL GOALS

From childhood all the way to adulthood, we have hopes and dreams. When we're younger, our goals are simpler and smaller – getting to eat what we want for dinner, buying a toy we want, or reading a certain book. As you grow older, your goals can become bigger and more long-term – getting into that sports team you've been training for, landing a college scholarship, starting a business, or finding a relationship.

Big dreams can be hard to conceptualize – and may be daunting when not broken down into smaller, more obtainable goals. For example, if your goal is to improve your chances of getting accepted into the college of your choice by the end of the school year, that big goal can be partitioned into smaller goals that are within your reach. You can set a goal to improve in one specific subject by Christmas, decide to take private lessons in another, and earn extra credit by joining a sports team or club.

Research shows that when faced with only one big task, people are less likely to complete it and more likely to despair than if faced with several, more accomplishable targets.

In addition, if your goals are too vague or general, even with the best of intentions, you might find yourself lost on the way to accomplishing them.

HERE ARE THE THREE TRICKS TO EFFECTIVE GOAL-SETTING:

- Have a clear, well-defined target.
- Break that target down into smaller goals.
- Make a plan and stick to it.

Effective goal-setting is an important skill, and one that encompasses in it other skills as well – such as time management, self-discipline, organization, and budgeting. You can read more about how to budget properly in chapter 18, *Planning a Budget*, and about managing your time in chapter 28, *Time Management*.

SET YOUR GOALS

It is important to be mindful and intentional about our goals. People need dreams and aspirations to keep them going, and accomplishments, however big or small, are part of what gives us purpose and satisfaction in life. That's part of the reason why people make New Year's resolutions – we all want to be better, happier, more successful, or more content with our lives. However, experience shows that the vast majority of these resolutions are not destined to last. The main reasons for people *not* sticking to their New Year's resolutions are that they set big, often unrealistic goals, don't know how to section them into achievable objectives, and don't take the time to make a detailed plan of action.

Write down your end goals in the exercise sheet at the end of this chapter. You can have one or many, they can be academic, social, financial, or personal, as long as they are authentic and realistic. Try to define them in more than one word or two. For example, a goal that might have looked like this in your head:

"have more money" should look more like this on the page: "earn a steady monthly income that surpasses my expenses by 10%", or "earn X sum of money by next January so that I can purchase my first car."

BREAK DOWN YOUR GOALS INTO SUB-GOALS

Next, try and analyze each goal you've written down and section it into smaller objectives. These are your sub-goals, which will help you on your way to your end goal. These targets should be feasible, simple, and limited by time. Following our previous example: "find a part-time job with a salary of $X per hour by the end of the month," "open a savings account and deposit X amount of money each month," "have a yard sale to earn money from all the things I don't use anymore but are in good condition within the next six months," etc., etc.

MAKE A PLAN

Finally, translate your sub-goals into actionable tasks and put them in a calendar. Give each task a target date that is realistic with your end goal and have your plan in a prominent place where you can look at it often. Forgotten dreams will never be realized, so having your goals at the front of your mind always will ensure that you are mindful about working towards them every day!

MY GOALS AND SUB-GOALS:

1 ....

    a. ....

    b. ....

    c. ....

    d. ....

    e. ....

2 ....

    a. ....

    b. ....

    c. ....

    d. ....

    e. ....

3 ....

    a. ....

    b. ....

    c. ....

    d. ....

    e. ....

CHAPTER 30:

REGULATING YOUR EMOTIONS

In our teen years, our bodies go through a lot of changes. Some of these changes are physical, others are hormonal or emotional. The hormonal changes that accompany puberty lead to real chemical imbalances in the brain, which often affect our mood and cause our emotions to shift easily.

Processing and channeling your emotions in a healthy way is a crucial skill for everyone, even for adults, but learning to do it as a teen can help you avoid frustration, anger, and depression, and focus instead on your hobbies and interests and on becoming a healthy, independent person.

Both biological (genetic) and environmental factors play a part in emotional regulation. The biological part is fixed and out of our control, but our environment is definitely something we have the power to influence, in all sorts of different ways.

HEALTHY HABITS FOR REGULATING EMOTIONS

- **GET ENOUGH SLEEP.** Sleep is crucial to our physical and mental health, and getting in the hours you need can do wonders for your day-to-day wellness. There is no fixed number of hours that is right for everyone, as each person has different energy and needs. However, the recommended amount of sleep for adolescents is between seven and nine hours each night, preferably the same hours each night. When we get into the habit of going to sleep and waking up at roughly the same time each day, we condition our brain to know which hours are meant for resting.

- **EXERCISE REGULARLY.** Exercise is great for your heart, lungs, and general physical health, but it is also an excellent remedy for stress, anxiety, and fatigue which in turn can aggravate emotional imbalance. Walking daily, going to the gym, or taking up sports is another healthy habit.

- **MEDITATE.** Meditation has been shown to strengthen brain function and improve focus and concentration. Dedicating half an hour or more each day to meditation is a good way to promote mental health, and a great opportunity to focus on yourself and your well-being without outside distractions. Meditation is also a study of breathing, and you can learn all sorts of techniques to help calm down. You can read more about this in chapter 32, *Meditation & Mindfulness*.

- **JOURNAL YOUR THOUGHTS AND FEELINGS.** Sometimes, the simple act of putting how you feel into words can lift a heavy weight off your shoulders. Journaling daily can help you sort out your emotions and understand how you're feeling and why, allowing you better control. Consider giving bullet journaling a try – this is more of a creative outlet and is not for everyone, but it can have amazing emotional benefits, too.

Balancing your emotions is definitely a challenge, but learning healthy coping mechanisms as a teen will pay off when you become a balanced adult with healthy control of your emotions!

CHAPTER 31:
CREATING A SUPPORT SYSTEM

Human beings are social creatures – we need regular interaction with family, friends, neighbors, colleagues, and even strangers to engage us and keep us happy.

These interactions can be positive, and they can sometimes be negative. The idea behind creating a support system in your life is detecting those positive relationships that make you happy, that lift you up and give you support and encouragement in what you do.

These connections are so important in this crucial stage of your life when you're developing into a young adult and finding your place in the world. In this chapter, you'll learn how to recognize your support system, whom to remove from it, and how to use it in times of need.

WHO IS IN YOUR SUPPORT SYSTEM?

Your network of support can be small or large – it can be one trusted parent, or a whole circle of family and friends, depending on your personal needs and circumstances. Think about the people who are most central and important in your life. Go through the list and ask yourself, would I go to this person in a time of need? Can I trust them to do what's best for me? Do I cherish them enough to do the same for them?

The people in your life whom you answered yes to all three questions about make up the core of your support system. These are the people who have your best interests at heart and whom you can completely trust to be by your side. They can be your parents or siblings, grandparents, aunts, uncles, or cousins, childhood friends, new friends, teachers or mentors, boyfriend or girlfriend, neighbors, and really anyone whose presence in your life is a positive, supportive one.

WHO SHOULD *NOT* BE PART OF YOUR SUPPORT SYSTEM?

There are people in your life, even people who are very close to you and you interact with them regularly, who may not fit the description above. That's fine, and it's okay to keep these people in your life and even interact with them regularly. However, it is important to know that however much you might love these people, the relationship you have with them is not enough for your support system. In times of need, in emergencies, or when you feel there is something you cannot handle alone, you might not be able to trust them to act in your favor.

While you analyze your connections in your mind, keep a sharp eye out for relationships that cross the line over to toxic. If there is anyone who makes you feel unsupported, demeaned, lied to, threatened, or abused in any way, recognize that this is a relationship better left behind. It is sometimes hard to cut ties with these people, as very often they are close friends, romantic partners, or even family members. Even if you cannot cut them completely out of your life, be wary of interacting with them and put your own well-being before your relationship with them when necessary.

HOW TO USE YOUR SUPPORT SYSTEM........

Your circle of support is there to help you when you need it. You may find that some people are better suited to help you in different kinds of situations – your dad might be the perfect person to go to when you have a problem that needs solving, while your best friend can be a shoulder to cry on.

Being aware and mindful of the people who make up your support system is crucial to your mental well-being. In emergencies, you will know immediately whom you can turn to without the risk of seeking help from someone unsuited to support you.

Remember that you make up other people's support systems too! Be mindful of who these people are, and be ready and willing to help them in their time of need, just as you hope that they would help you.

CHAPTER 32:
MEDITATION AND MINDFULNESS

Mindfulness is the art of self-awareness and attention to the present. It is all about being in the moment, being attuned to yourself and your surroundings, and concentrating on what matters most. Many cultures around the world recognize the healing benefits of being mindful of oneself and as such incorporate certain practices into daily life, and it has been shown to be greatly effective in dealing with stress, anxiety, or emotions that are out of balance – as many teens' emotions are, due to the extensive physical and hormonal changes that accompany puberty.

Mindfulness is a state of mind, one that can be achieved in several ways, including meditation. Meditation forces one to stop, reflect, and concentrate on the heart, the mind, and the body. It cultivates skills like effective breathing and self-control, can improve self-esteem, memory, and concentration, and has been shown to be beneficial to both physical and mental health.

Meditation is something that you can practice regularly, or only in certain situations when you feel the need. Like any other skill, it is something that is learned and honed with time, so the more you do it – the more natural and easier it will become. Some people spend many years dedicating their life to mastering the art of meditation.

WHAT IS MEDITATION?

Meditation is practiced by many religions, the most prominent of them being Buddhism and Hinduism. Today, it is widely used in the Western world as well to reduce stress and anxiety and even as a treatment for mental health issues such as depression.

There are different ways to meditate, but most include allocating a designated amount of time to sitting alone in a quiet place near the ground and concentrating on your breathing for the length of the meditation.

The purpose is to try to clear your mind of thoughts and distractions and focus on just being where you are, inhaling and exhaling.

HOW TO START MEDITATING

There are plenty of guides and programs you can find online to help you start meditating, but as a complete beginner try to start by simply dedicating five minutes every day to breathing. Organize a comfortable place to sit, make sure your environment is free of distractions, and choose a time when you're not likely to be needed for anything urgently.

You can play soft, calming music quietly in the background, and wear clothes that are comfortable to sit in.

Spend the first minute concentrating on your body – mentally scan your body and relax your limbs and joints one by one, until everything is loose. Then, spend three minutes focusing solely on your breathing – in and out. Let your lungs fill with air completely before you exhale, and let them empty before you take air back in. For the last minute, let the breathing come naturally and try to clear your mind entirely.

See how you feel once the five minutes are over. The first few times will probably be challenging, but with time you should be feeling more relaxed, at ease with yourself, and refreshed after each session. Try increasing the time or frequency, and experiment with different times of day to see which works best for you.

PART 7:

WORKING

CHAPTER 33:
WRITING A RÉSUMÉ

As a teenager, you are starting to become more independent. You might take on more responsibilities at home or at school, and in general, you are freer to make your own choices than you were as a child.

A big part of gaining independence is finding a job. Not only will working provide you with valuable experience for the future, but it will also grant you an income that is entirely your own. Whether you want to save for college or simply want some spending money of your own, the first step towards finding a job is writing your résumé.

A résumé is a short document, usually up to a page long, which includes all the information about you that could be relevant for a potential employer or hiring manager to know.

As a teen looking for your first "real" job, you may not have much to put on a résumé, but there are tricks to make your résumé stand out among others.

WHAT IS INCLUDED IN A RÉSUMÉ?............

- **PERSONAL DETAILS:** At the top of the page, put your full name and your address.
- **CONTACT INFORMATION:** Your phone number and e-mail address, so that hiring managers can get in touch with you.
- **EDUCATION AND QUALIFICATIONS:** List the name of your high school and your (expected) graduation year. If

you have a GED, put that down too. If not, you can include your GPA. Include your major if it is related to the job you are applying for.

Also include any and all school activities and accomplishments, such as Honor Roll or school awards.

If you are a college student, list the name of your college and your expected graduation year.

- **QUALIFICATIONS:** If you have taken any extracurricular or out-of-school courses or training, you can list these too, including the name of the establishment and details of any certificate you may have received.

- **EXPERIENCE:** This section is where potential employers look for information on previous jobs and titles you've held to gauge your experience. This is where things might get tricky, as you may not have much work experience to lean on.

  If you have worked before, even informally as a babysitter, tutor, etc., be sure to include these jobs here. Add details about the responsibilities you had and the skills you acquired.

  In addition to work, you can add extracurricular activities you led or participated in at school, such as committees, clubs, sports teams, student government, events you planned, etc. This can show a future employee that you are well-rounded, hardworking, and take initiative.

- **SKILLS:** This is the place to write down any other abilities you may have that could help you excel at the job you're applying for. This could be computer proficiency, programming, graphic design, leadership, problem-solving, customer service, etc. Remember that anything a hiring manager reads in your résumé can come up in a subsequent interview, so only list skills that you feel comfortable elaborating on.

- **LANGUAGES:** Another section that can be found on most résumés is the language section, although some people include this information under "skills". Here, note the language or languages you speak, and your level of proficiency. Use these levels as a guide:

    Intermediate – you can understand and participate in basic conversation, but not well enough to converse freely.

    Advanced – you can carry out full conversations but speaking the language does not come completely naturally and you may lack some vocabulary or have an imperfect grasp of the grammar.

    Proficient – you speak the language fluently, though it is not your mother tongue.

    Native – this is your native language, which you have spoken from birth. If you are bilingual, list both languages as native.

HOW TO DESIGN A RÉSUMÉ

Résumés should be visually pleasing, so don't just type everything out in black and white. There are plenty of resources online where you can find free downloadable résumé templates, or you can design your own.

KEEP THESE GUIDELINES IN MIND:

- Choose a font that looks professional and is easy to read. Avoid cursive or childish fonts.

- Make sure your résumé is in a printable format and mobile-friendly.

- Choose a color scheme that is minimalistic and professional-looking.

- Keep it short and to the point – your résumé should not exceed one page.

CHAPTER 34:

ACING AN INTERVIEW

After perfecting your CV, it's time to start applying for job positions. In addition to a résumé with appropriate credentials, most jobs will require an interview (or more than one) before they accept candidates.

It doesn't matter if you're applying for a retail job, a job in the food industry, or an internship – you want to ace your interview and leave your interviewer with a great impression that will stand out among the pool of candidates they are sure to meet.

DO YOUR HOMEWORK

Before your interview, put some time and effort into researching the company, its values, and its history. This will both help you see how good a fit the job is for you and will demonstrate that you are thorough and resourceful, two positive qualities in a potential hire.

You can use Google to search for information or even visit the business's location to scout out its work environment and current focus. Contacting current or former employees, if you know any, is also a great way to gain insight into the job you're pursuing.

The job description you originally responded to might also hold clues as to the kind of employee the business is looking for. In addition to experience and skills, it may list qualities and other requirements that you can use to your benefit during the interview.

BE PREPARED

Spend some time thinking about answers to questions you may be asked in an interview and write them down to go over again several times before the interview. Even ask a family member or a friend to sit with you and simulate a job interview. If you've practiced beforehand, expressing yourself will come easier in real time.

THESE ARE SOME COMMON INTERVIEW QUESTIONS YOU CAN PREPARE FOR IN ADVANCE:

- **WHICH RELEVANT EXPERIENCE DO YOU HAVE?**

    List any previous experience that may give you an advantage over other candidates. You don't necessarily need to have worked in the same job or industry, but you might have worked or volunteered somewhere that taught you to be organized, or improved your ability to manage, and so on.

- **WHAT ARE YOUR STRENGTHS AND WEAKNESSES?**

    When listing your strengths, choose qualities that are relevant to the job you are after. These can be things like responsibility, thoroughness, work ethic, quick learning, etc. Leave out personal strengths that will not be an asset in the workplace.

    Similarly, when listing your weaknesses, avoid anything that might diminish your ability to do the job you are applying for. Opt for real weaknesses you see in yourself, which should be minimally detrimental to your character in the workplace.

- **WHAT WILL YOU CONTRIBUTE TO THIS WORKPLACE?**

    Your answer should convince the interviewer that you would be a real asset to the team. This is the place to point out any unique attributes, personality traits, and experience which would make you a perfect fit for the job.

- **TELL ME ABOUT A TIME WHEN YOU...**

    Your interviewer might want to hear about challenges you've overcome, successes you've experienced, times you've failed, projects you've led, etc. It can be difficult to remember these things when you're put on the spot, so try to think of a few interesting stories from your past experience to have ready.

MAKE AN IMPRESSION

How you look is a big part of the first impression you make. In fact, first impressions are believed to be formed within the first few seconds of meeting someone, which will often be over before you've even had a chance to open your mouth and introduce yourself.

- **DRESS SMART** – even if the job is in a casual setting, looking sharp at the interview is important. Avoid T-shirts and ripped or overly revealing clothes and put an effort into making your outfit look professional.

- **BE WELL-MANNERED** – shake your interviewer's hand, smile, and speak politely. Sit up straight and look them in the eyes, pay close attention to what is said, and show that you are pleasant to be around, an essential thing for an employer to see.

Remember – any interview, even an unsuccessful one, is an opportunity to learn! Ask for feedback or simply debrief yourself afterward, thinking about what you might do better next time.

CHAPTER 35:
KNOWING YOUR RIGHTS AT WORK

After perfecting your résumé, acing your interviews, and finally starting a new job, it's important to know what your rights are as an employee. It can be easy to take advantage of younger workers who are unaware of what is or isn't required of them, but being informed of your rights in the workplace can make the experience of your first job far more enjoyable and fair.

BASIC RIGHTS

However old you are and wherever you're employed, you are entitled to some basic rights as an employee.

- You have a right to privacy and should not be forced to divulge information that is not relevant to your work. This goes for intrusive questions that may be asked during interviews, as well. Employers may use surveillance to monitor your use of your phone during work hours, it is not in their right to see or disclose the private conversations you hold with others.

- If you work at mealtimes, your employer should provide appropriate breaks. The time you take for meals may be deducted from your salary, but you should still have the opportunity to take those breaks when you need them.

WAGE AND PAYMENT

Your contract should denote your wage, the hours you are required to work, and the conditions of your payment.

- Minimum wage is a requirement by law. Do not agree to work for less than the minimum wage.

- Withholding payment from a worker is illegal. Your employer should pay you your full wage promptly and without delay, per the agreement stated in your contract.

- Unless specifically agreed otherwise, you should be compensated for any overtime you work. If you see that putting in extra hours goes unrecognized, you can refuse to work more than the hours you are paid for.

- If your contract includes benefits such as health insurance, PTO (paid time off), a retirement plan, etc., you have the right to make sure you receive those, too.

HEALTH AND SAFETY AT WORK

Your employer is obligated to provide a safe work environment for all employees.

- Any protective gear or equipment must be provided or funded by your employer.

- If you sense that any element of your job poses an immediate threat to your life or health, physical or mental, you have the right to refuse to do the work until the problem has been resolved.

- Your workplace should be clean and any potential safety hazards dealt with immediately.

- Your employer must keep you informed about safety procedures and is responsible for making sure you know what to do in an emergency.

SEXUAL HARASSMENT AND DISCRIMINATION AT WORK

You spend a significant amount of time at your workplace, and as such, it should afford you a safe, comfortable, and discrimination-free environment.

- If someone at work, be they your supervisor, co-worker, or even subordinate, is behaving in a way that makes you feel threatened or uncomfortable, report them. It is your employer's responsibility to prevent sexual harassment and bullying in the workplace. Know that you can take legal action if the problem is ignored or dismissed.

- If you feel discriminated against at work because of your gender, race, color, religion, disability, etc., report the discrimination to your supervisor or HR officer.

- Legally, you cannot be penalized or fired for lodging a complaint about harassment or discrimination you experience at work.

CHAPTER 36:

STARTING A BUSINESS

The term "a business" can sound like a big thing that is far out of your reach. But when you think about it, almost every big business and institution started as a small venture or an idea in someone's head. Even the lemonade stand you had as a child was a sort of business, and that kid who sold hairclips or chocolate bars at school was a businessperson, too.

Entrepreneurship is the act of initiating and promoting a business venture from an idea to reality. Anyone can be an entrepreneur, as long as they have the creativity to come up with a new idea, the time and resources to make it happen, and the patience and self-discipline to persevere.

Many famous entrepreneurs started in their teens – Mark Zuckerberg founded Facebook at age 19, Fred DeLuca was 17 when he started Subway, and the successful bath bomb brand Da Bomb was started by sisters Isabel and Caroline Bercaw when they were only 16 and 15 years old.

Your teenage years, when you are mostly free of financial obligations and have sufficient time to invest in an idea, are an excellent time to put that entrepreneurial mind to work!

CHOOSE SOMETHING YOU'RE PASSIONATE ABOUT

Don't try to think about what will earn you the most money or what will be most successful. These are important factors in starting a business, but true success is built on passion. Making an idea come to fruition takes time and effort, and a project you aren't passionate and excited about is destined to fail.

You may be passionate about a hobby like baking or reading, you may get excited when you talk about global warming or women's rights, or you might just love animals and everything to do with them. Channel your passion into an idea for a business venture that you believe in and will truly enjoy.

ADDRESS A PROBLEM OR NEED

A successful product or business is one that provides a solution to a problem or plays to people's needs or desires. Channel your passion to fill one of these requirements and you're looking at a realistic idea that has true business potential. The Bercaw sisters' bath bombs with a surprise inside didn't solve a problem for anyone – but they appealed to people's desires and their love of whimsy, which is why they were so successful (in addition, of course, to the hard work they put into starting their company).

ACQUIRE FUNDING

Different-sized projects require different funding, but the chances are you'll need at least some money to take off before your venture is earning you an income. Investigate your funding options – do you have savings you can use? Do you have a steady income in the form of a salary or allowance? Is there someone who can help you finance your idea? You can always try crowdfunding if you believe that your idea is strong enough to appeal to a large market.

GIVE IT YOUR ALL

No idea has made it big without someone putting in days and nights to make it work. If you're working on something you're truly passionate about, find the self-discipline and time to give it everything you have. Businesses don't build themselves and just think how proud you will be one day when you look back and see how much work you put into something that you can honestly call your own.

CONCLUSION

If you've reached the end of this book, whether you've read every word or jumped between the chapters you thought would benefit you most, we're happy to have been able to provide you with some essential life skills as you set out to face the big wide world.

There is so much to learn about life and so many skills that you have yet to master on your own, but we believe that the skills thoughtfully and simply laid out in this book are an invaluable source of knowledge for young people. You are just starting your life – starting to learn who you are, to understand what you like and what kind of choices you should make, and perhaps making plans and dreams for your future. We hope that this book has taken you to a great starting point, and made you feel capable and confident in your abilities.

We know that growing up can sometimes come with pressure, anxiety, and a lot of uncertainty. It's important to remember that there are people around you who want the best for you – and can help you manage these feelings. After all, every adult was in your position once; excited to discover what the world has to offer, but perhaps unsure just how to start.

We ask that you take what you've learned from this book and use it to do good. Be a responsible citizen, a healthy and well-balanced adult, a socially active and thoughtful human. You can keep *Essential Life Skills for Teen Girls* handy for whenever you need to go back and refresh your memory on how to regulate your emotions, what the deal is with insurance, how to do the laundry, or what the correct steps are for sewing a button.

We hope you've enjoyed this book and that it continues to be your guide, lighting your way through those wonderful teenage years.

THANK YOU SO MUCH FOR READING!

We'd appreciate your help and support so that we can keep bringing you more beautiful content like this, so if you could go to Amazon and leave us a review we'd be so grateful!

ABOUT
MADE EASY PRESS

At MADE EASY PRESS, our goal is to bring you beautifully designed, thoughtful gifts and products.

We strive to make complicated things – easy. Whether it's learning new skills or putting memories into words, our books are led by values of family, creativity, and self-care and we take joy in creating authentic experiences that make people truly happy.

Look out for other books by MADE EASY PRESS here!

ABOUT THE AUTHOR

DANI SILAS wrote the *Essential Life Skills* series to help kids and teens acquire the self-confidence and independence to be the best they can be.

She believes that while school can teach you many important things, the *most* important things you can learn in life are the ones you learn outside the classroom. That's why the *Essential Life Skills* books are packed full of information, tips, and practical advice on everything from cooking and cleaning to social skills and handling money.

Dani loves to read and spend time with her husband and their dog, Amy. She studied psychology and linguistics and some of her favorite things are sunshine, Harry Potter, art, baking, and crafting.

www.ingramcontent.com/pod-product-compliance
Lightning Source LLC
LaVergne TN
LVHW022233080526
838199LV00106B/332